"Ted Kooser is kind, as we know from every essay and poem published in this volume to honor the poet's retirement from the University of Nebraska. Ted Kooser is accomplished and beloved as teacher, writer, poet, editor, painter and friend. And Ted Kooser leaves the public life of the university as a national poet laureate and Pulitzer Prize winner to become what he has always been, a private man of genius. Long may he thrive and publish, labor in his fields, make and paint the bird houses that adorn our trees, the gorgeous chicken coop in his yard, and write poems so distilled that our souls bend in delight."

   —Hilda Raz, author of *Letter from a Place I've Never Been: New and Collected Poems, 1986–2020*

"I think Ted's *Lights on a Ground of Darkness* is one of the most exquisite slim memoirs ever written on this earth. And that is what seems needed in our world. More lights. More care. On our big shared beautiful ground of darkness."

   —Naomi Shihab Nye, author of *Cast Away: Poems for Our Time*

"Ted Kooser must be the most accessible and enjoyable major poet in America."

   —Michael Dirda, *Washington Post*

"Ted Kooser is an American original, whose work in poetry is akin to the paintings of Grant Wood and the music of Aaron Copland."

   —*Kenyon Review*

"He is one of our best poets, and not simply because his style widens the reach of the art form."

   —Nick Ripatrazone, *National Review*

"Kooser's greatest assets have long been his generous eye and his way with understatement."

—*New York Times*

"The librarian of Congress has pointed out that Kooser is 'the first poet laureate chosen from the Great Plains.' And not merely from, but of. In a poetry world dominated by poets who frequently shift from academic job to job and region to region, Kooser's poetry is rare for its sense of being so firmly and enduringly rooted in one locale."

—Brad Leithauser, *New York Times*

"[Ted Kooser] knows more about small-town people than any other poet I know; he's a truly American poet."

—William Cole, former columnist for the *Saturday Review*

"Kooser is a poet by nature, and his essays have the generous feel of a man who's rolled up his sleeves, pen in hand, for a long time, choosing words as an act of beauty, and knowing the small things of the world are of great import."

—The *Bloomsbury Review*

"[*Local Wonders*] is a heartfelt plainspoken book about slowing down and appreciating the world around you."

—*New York Times* book critic Janet Maslin on CBS *News Sunday Morning*

"[Reading] *Local Wonders* is a bit like running into Lao Tsu and Confucius in line at the hardware store. A Taoist love of country life permeates the book. . . . It is not nature alone, Kooser's beautiful book reminds us, but the play of the imagination on nature—the mind that can speculate on the connection between stars and moths—that produces glory and brings insight into life's inescapable truths."

 —*Fourth Genre*

"Ted Kooser's *Local Wonders* is the quietest magnificent book I've ever read."

 —Jim Harrison, author of *Legends of the Fall*

More in Time

More in Time

A TRIBUTE TO TED KOOSER

EDITED BY Jessica Poli, Marco Abel,
and Timothy Schaffert

UNIVERSITY OF NEBRASKA PRESS | *Lincoln*

Library of Congress Control Number: 2020949590

Set in ITC New Baskerville by A. Shahan.

Contents

Editorial Note

One fine pre-COVID-19 evening, while enjoying a cocktail or three, two of us—Marco and Timothy—discussed the amazing productivity of the creative writing faculty and graduate students in our department, the English Department at the University of Nebraska. We also discussed a course in development: "Literary Nebraska," which features multiple lectures on the subject of Nebraska's contributions, past and present, to the national literary panorama. Noting the impending retirement of one of the pillars of our faculty, and a key figure in this panorama ("He *is* Mr. Literary Nebraska," one of our colleagues had remarked), we got the vague idea of finding an appropriate way to honor him. This colleague, of course, is two-term U.S. Poet Laureate and Pulitzer Prize–winning poet Ted Kooser. Thinking of Ted's role not only as a member of our faculty but also in the larger community throughout the Midwest and across the country, we soon landed on the possibility of coediting a volume of contributions from many of Ted's colleagues, including former graduate students. While our idea was initially inspired by the German tradition of the *Festschrift*—a publication honoring a respected academic by bringing together contributions from a range of the honoree's former students and colleagues—we quickly reconceived our effort, deciding that it would be much better to honor Ted by inviting our contributors not only to submit their own creative pieces but also to reflect on how they respond to or are inspired by Ted and his work.

This decision, in turn, made it clear to us that we really would need a practicing poet to collaborate with us on this project: enter Jessica. As a former student of Ted's, she helped us think about the role of Ted's "tutorials" in our concept for the book.

Every fall semester, Ted met one-on-one with his students in sessions that were more than just workshops; many students found them to be as therapeutic as they were instructive, Ted's warmth and instincts having a profound influence on how they approached not only their work but also their lives as poets. We quickly realized that the contributions from Ted's former students about their experiences in these tutorials would be one of our book's unique features. Indeed, of the sixty-eight contributions included in *More in Time*—a phrase Ted has been known to use when signing off his emails, as James Crews explains in an essay that corresponds to his wonderful poem, "More in Time: A Letter to Ted"—more than a quarter explicitly relate their creative contributions to Ted's teaching. We believe that these pieces offer valuable insights into Ted's remarkable abilities as a teacher of poetry writing and that they also shed useful light on how creative writing is an effect of the development of an author's craft. It is this craft that creative writing students in our department hone en route to earning their PhD, which culminates in a creative dissertation. These accounts of Ted's tutorials invite readers to note not only the consistency with which Ted has taught generation after generation of our students but also the subtle differences that emerge in them—small changes in his pedagogical approach that cumulatively reveal the *craft* that is involved in the teaching of creative writing as practiced by a master tutor such as Ted.

We started this project in the midst of the COVID-19 pandemic and were therefore not sure how many writers we could persuade to contribute. But—and we say this without taking poetic license—it took only a few hours after sending out our initial email soliciting contributions for us to realize just how immensely eager Ted's former students, his colleagues, and, in many cases, his friends were to be included in this project. Each response we received communicated genuine enthusiasm for being given the opportunity to contribute to a project about and inspired by Ted's work as both poet and teacher, the core of which might be the very demonstration that attending to the nuances of the everyday is capable of transcending the authentic material particularities of the ordinary and thereby rendering sensible—that is, allowing our sense perceptions to notice and our mind to make sense of, to understand—a common that is open-ended. This common—maybe better: this *sensus communis*—is open-ended because it is not tied (as is the private and the public) to property, including to the property of the individual and of the (lyrical) "I": of *i*dentity. This open-endedness of Ted's poetics and teaching, as became apparent to us, is capable of calling forth, or into being, poetic responses from others because they feel invited—truly *welcomed*—by his poetics to respond. Ted's poetics, then, communicates a sense of hospitality, one that exists because of, and consists of, his use of language. It exists in his language and indeed, for his interlocutors, in the world. It is this world—this *sensus communis* produced by Ted's poetics—that his interlocutors expand through their responses; and in so doing, they also subtly alter the very *sense* of the common that Ted's poetry evokes.

Perhaps we can say, then, that Ted's work performatively hails future poetic expressions—expressions that will take their cue from (and return to) but also (necessarily) go beyond the material world his poetry so compellingly describes and, by describing it so precisely, transforms. That is, these poetic expressions responding to Ted's work take their cue from his poetry. But in so doing, they not only return to his poetics (though they frequently do this as well) but also go beyond the very world in which Ted's poetry is grounded, as we can see especially in those poetic responses in this volume that feel invited to talk back—to engage in a mode of response that, importantly, manifests itself in these interlocutors' hands not as rejection (a dialectical "no") but instead as an affirmation of sorts: a self-confident insistence on adding to the place-based *sensus communis* that Ted's language delineates.

Last but not least, the particular, meticulous description of the ordinariness of the world Ted's poetry describes—its mundaneness—transforms that world, we think, precisely because of the linguistic translation of that world. It renders this ordinariness noticeable, imaginable, seeable, perceivable *to others*. In a way, the ordinary, in and through Ted's poetic hands, is made to enter the "distribution of the sensible," to use a famous philosophical phrase: it is allowed to enter the framework of "common sense"—that is, of our sense perceptions that otherwise often exclude precisely what is described in Ted's poems because of the fact that it often is not deemed noteworthy. It is this transformative aspect of his work—transformative because it happens *in* and *through* his poetic articulation of the everyday—that, notwithstanding its exceedingly meticulous attention to place, ultimately locates his poetics as one of temporality. It is a poetics that offers readers, precisely by enhancing or intensifying their affective responsiveness to the world, the promise that there will be more to come. It promises us that the common is expandable, that the common *will* be expanded not least since, unlike both the private and the public, it is not limited by scarcity. In short, one might say that Ted's poetics offers a measure of hope to his readers precisely because it promises them that in the here and now of the everyday there will be more to come, that there will be *more in time*.

Marco, on behalf of the editorial team

Acknowledgments

We would like to thank the University of Nebraska Press for its support of this project and in particular Bridget Barry for responding so favorably when we approached her with our idea, Emily Wendell for helping us secure permissions to reprint several poems, Joeth Zucco for ushering this project through the copyediting process, and Karen Hardy Brown for expertly copyediting the manuscript. We couldn't have wished for a more appropriate publisher for this project. We are also grateful to Jonis Agee for providing support and insight and the Rahl Foundation for the Arts for its assistance. We especially want to thank Patricia Emile, the long-term assistant editor for Ted's American Life in Poetry column, for giving us a long list of suggestions for possible contributors; we are delighted to say that almost all of them are featured in the following pages. Speaking of contributors: we are truly grateful to everyone who is included in this book and can honestly say that the enthusiasm with which everyone replied to our request for submissions gave us the fuel to put this volume together in a mere four months. We could not have done it without you all! Last but not least, we of course want to thank Ted himself—for the collegiality and kindness he's shown to us (as well as our colleagues) over all these years; for all the work he's done for the world of poetry in the Midwest and beyond; and for his longstanding generous support of the English Department at the University of Nebraska, not least of our undergraduate and graduate students.

Introduction: *Splitting an Order,* Ted Kooser, Copper Canyon, 2017

DIANE GLANCY

In the title poem of his book *Splitting an Order,* Kooser writes of an old couple in a small café. The man cleans his glasses before he cuts a cold roast-beef sandwich in half. No pickles or onions. Just plain meat and bread. The man hands the half to his wife, who unrolls her napkin and places her spoon, knife, and fork in order, which she does not need to eat a sandwich half. But the order of what one does to prepare to eat is there.

The poem is fourteen lines, the act of a sonnet that doesn't fit the sonnet world, yet continues as though it does. What difference, a few rhymes, a few metrics? The volta, the turning, the splitting from the order of things, is there. It is not the hardship, but the humanity, the relationship of the two that carries the weight, the meaning of the poem.

An extended, unrhyming, unmetered sonnet about the detailed act of a man caring for his wife. Whether they share a meal because of limited funds, or because the desire for food sometimes lessens as one ages, they eat a smaller lunch. Maybe the trip to the café in town is an outing for the sake of being out of the house. Of being in public. Surrounded with others as if from an isolated farmhouse on the Nebraska prairie.

"I like to watch," Kooser begins the poem. A habit of the poet. His observation. His ability to write what he sees. To narrate the splitting of an order. Always splitting. From the observable to what he thinks about what he has observed. Splitting from the seen to the unseen thoughts in his head.

Listen to what he says about the moon in "New Moon": "How much it must bear on its back." A "great ball." A "blue shadow." "I want to be better at carrying sorrow." His face "a mask, formed over the shadows that fill me." There is voltaic direction—his poem travels as current (not erratically) but with purpose as he splits the shadow from the object of which it is a shadow to make an object of it. (If my Voltammeter is working.)

I am in Texas while writing this. My library is in my house in Kansas. I also am without internet in the place where I am staying. The library in the small town is closed because of the pandemic. I drove forty miles to the Barnes and Noble in Denton. One book by Kooser was there, *Splitting an Order*, which I bought and read and reread, thinking the part could serve for the whole. I write an introduction to his work by perusing one volume of it because my other volumes are 482 miles to the north. In this time of isolation, of being made smaller, of experiencing a narrowing of possibilities of what I can do each day, the snippet of Kooser's work spoke the largeness of the world. It split the order of my experience.

I decide one book can speak for Kooser. It uncovers what I would call "salt of the earth." Thought and emotion. Cadence. Image. The sky and the land upon which it sits. A prairie lyric. The importance of order to be examined. Explicated. Made something of.

In "Potatoes," the "sepia-and-green" in the first line becomes an old photograph. The steel disk of the horse-drawn two-wheeled planter is tactile. The horse "was brown as varnish / as it pulled us forward, all / of us, with black clay dropping / from its shoes." There is an ekphrastic quality to Kooser's poems. A joining of the visual image and the idea conveyed in language—splitting the order of things. His work pulling forward as if a draft horse.

"Gabardine" is a poem that observes men talking—possibly, I imagine, along a bench at the feed store. Gabardine is a coarse cloth. Not a fabric usually worn in our current age. It also has a split meaning. Gabardine is to wander about, to travel. To pilgrimage. Another poem with old men in it—old men talking as birds flying up. Then settling again between points of conversations. The poem also works as a two-wheeled planter that opens the earth and closes it again when the seed potato has been planted.

There is a broad sweep in Kooser's work. Maybe because of the largeness of the land he inhabits. I notice in "Garrison, Nebraska" he mentions the white caps of snow. There is something of the ocean on the Great Plains. An ocean used to be there. Maybe the land remembers, and Kooser picked up the land's thoughts as he wrote.

I just finished writing about the Old Testament Job who takes three chapters to talk about himself. Then God takes four chapters to say what he has done, beginning with "Where were you when I laid the foundations of the earth?" After which Job understands his place in the chain of being, an outdated term for relativists, but a term that still seems to have some bearing in God's world. If you believe in God's world.

I like to be pulled off-course by the impact of Kooser's poems. His beam splitter that seems to focus on the human heart—the pumping of life blood—of meaning—of significance. Of valor in the face of battle, which every poem is—when it comes to capturing the essence of what one faces.

In "Estate Sale," Kooser seems to play with iambic fragments, almost reaching them, yet splits from—

the board / where birds sat down to eat (I removed "the" from before "birds" to make my point)
where glass once fit (I removed "the" from before "glass")
a few seeds missed by mice (I removed "the" from before "mice")
the pale wings stiffly folded.
An empty coffee can
In this poor urn, the peonies / rode

I like this undercurrent, this cellar. This rhythm split from the exact metric of a form poem.

Kooser's work is narrative. Removed from the formalistic that would be a relationship that doesn't quite fit—to capture the raw world in its radiance. I want to be in this world that is cared for by the poet's hand. I want to see what I would pass over without consideration. Without mulling. He's on a roll holding a tin potato bin—holding seed potatoes—holding my attention. Opening the earth and folding it back under once the seed potato has been planted. He exposes and closes again within soil of language. Seeing the inner workings, feeling the steel disc roll along our understanding. Like Job, realizing the order of things. A dignity in the stripping. An integrity in the grit. It is poetry's job to confront. To upturn. To implant the ordinary with the seed potatoes, which is interpretation of the place we inhabit. An important line in the Old Testament Book of Job—Can the rush grow up without the mire?—Job 8:11. Can the plant thrive without the nutrients of the soil and the rain and the sunlight? What if we are God's plants rooted in the mire for our own good? For our growth?

"The Rollerblader" again begins with the act of observation. "I saw her coming from a long way off." The whisk broom—movement—does she even know what a whisk broom is?

Kooser's poems are correspondences with which one can look at matters with genuine empathy for the world and us in it. Overwhelmed at times, but hemmed with the strict going on of the moon, of the seasons, of human life itself. It is in the seeming inertia of the moon and the long list of objects at the estate sale on their migrational path contrasted with the lovely fury of the rollerblader—all these images from different poems roll into one another—gaining momentum as they roll us into Kooser's dynamic world. Rollerblade also reminds me of the blade on the planter—the raw blade of language. Splitting the order. That's how we endure.

Ted Kooser served as the thirteenth Poet Laureate of the United States (2004–6), a consultant to the Library of Congress. He has a long list of published books. A longer list of honors and awards. He was Presidential Professor at the University of Nebraska. A man who does his job writing and teaching and being a Human Being—which is what human beings should attain to as we continue our journey.

I wonder if it was Kooser or the publisher who chose an austere cover for the book, Stephen Dinsmore's *Objects on a Gray Table*, for it carries the tone of the book. I wonder who decided which poem would bear the title of the book, *Splitting an Order*, for it is prophetic. It reveals poetry's duty to disrupt. To see inside. To state. Witness. Record. Shape. Preserve.

Another poem, "Snapshot," gets back to visual art of the land—the representational. The penmanship of light. The shadows through blinds. Both are given. Both are received. I can say again, the order of our world has been split. Get used to it. It seems to be the way things move.

In this time of pandemic when it seems we have half a plain roast-beef sandwich—when we have a curfew of activity—a smaller lunch, so to speak—we have the subtle voltage of Kooser's language to frame it—to make endurable the distances that exist between us.

More in Time

Ted Kooser Is My President

When I travel abroad, I will invoke
Ted's poems at checkpoints:
yes, barns, yes, memory, gentility,
the quiet little wind among stones.
If they ask, You are American?
I will say, Ted's kind of American.
No, I carry no scissors or matches.
Yes, horizons, dinner tables.
Yes, weather, the honesty of it.
Buttons, chickens. Feel free
to dump my purse. I'll wander
to the window, stare out for days.
Actually, I have never been
to Nebraska, except with Ted,
who hosted me dozens of times,
though we have never met.
His deep assurance comforts me.
He's not big on torture at all.
He could probably sneak into your country
when you weren't looking
and say something really good about it.
Have you noticed those purple blossoms
in a clump beside your wall?

. . .

When frustrated with politics, I have always turned to poetry.
Back during the George W. Bush administration, I read *Delights
& Shadows* by Ted Kooser with grateful desperation, and this
poem was born. Later I would meet Ted and work for two very

happy weeks as visiting writer at the University of Nebraska. This poem came back into my mind even more strongly during the bizarre political nightmare that succeeded President Obama's administration. Poems sometimes remake themselves, even for the author. Ted was my president once, and he could be again. Also, I think Ted's *Lights on a Ground of Darkness* is one of the most exquisite slim memoirs ever written on this earth. And that is what seems needed in our world. More lights. More care. On our big shared beautiful ground of darkness.

What Ted Likes

When I knocked on his office door at 8:00 a.m. each Monday, Ted often peeled that morning's poem off the printer, as though we'd just have a little exchange—a first draft from the Pulitzer Prize–winning, two-term poet laureate, and a paltry offering from his nervous grad student. He arrived around six to squeeze in writing time before meeting individually with graduate students for his tutorials.

One Monday, he waved me in, handing over a poem about repairing his roof while his dog, Howard, waited below. "Do you think this is too sentimental?" he asked.

I settled into the comfy chair next to his desk. Who was I to say anything Ted Kooser wrote was sentimental? Back then I could barely tell a sonnet from a simile. I don't remember what I said. Probably something wishy-washy like, "I don't know. I like the dog and how you're both getting up there in years, both worried about each other."

Ted listened, nodded. "Let's see what you have."

I fished a list poem out of my notebook. An experiment. I didn't think Ted would like it. He seemed to like poems of close observation, where the speaker is not too focused on the self, the kind of poems I wrote with him in mind, hoping he'd say, *This is good.*

I was not alone in seeking Ted's approval. At a Halloween party that Saturday, grad student poets decked out in ragtag costumes had gathered in the kitchen of a 1940s bungalow south of campus. A beagle, a nun, Death, Lady Gaga, a couple Lord of the Rings characters, and I compared notes on Ted's tutorial.

The beagle, who in real life wrote mostly fiction, confessed, "I don't think Ted likes my poems. Too many characters. He says I should keep them to under a handful."

"You're too used to writing short stories," Death said. "Try writing about nature. Ted likes nature poems."

"Or food," the nun offered. "Ted likes poems about food."

Lady Gaga swirled the ice in her Moscow Mule. "It's not so much about the food as the people eating the food. Ted likes poems about family."

"As long as you keep 'em short," Lord of the Rings said.

The other Lord of the Rings disagreed. "No, he likes long poems."

Raggedy Anne wandered over. Her wig of bright red yarn tilted to one side. "What are we talking about?"

"We're trying to figure out what kind of poetry Ted likes," I said.

"Oh, that's easy," she said, tugging her pigtails. "Metaphor. He likes poems with a singular, apt metaphor."

The conversation replayed in my head as Ted read my list poem. I tried to remember how many "characters" I'd included. It wasn't a nature poem exactly, nor a food poem, though Cap'n Crunch, chocolate, and potato chips made appearances. At least the poem was about family. But was there a metaphor?

Ted cleared his throat and began, "You know, Jill."

I prepared myself for disappointment. No doubt, he would protect my feelings, saying something gentle like, *I see what you're trying to do here*, or, *Have you considered another form for this?* He'd never started with those words before—*You know, Jill*—but I could imagine them followed by words I feared, saying the poem seemed *contrived, self-pitying*, or *too clever*. Instead, what he said was, "You know, Jill, this is quite good." He made suggestions, of course, which I furiously scribbled in my notebook, including, "It would help to know what age you are here."

The word he used most was "authentic." He found my poem *authentic*. We talked about death, loss, suicide, and mystery. The big subjects. The ones that prove difficult to write about in an original way without becoming what I'd feared my poem was—contrived, self-pitying, and clever—and what he'd feared his poem was: sentimental.

Over the next few weeks, his students and I stopped talking about what Ted likes and trying to write toward it. One of the things Ted did in his tutorial, something he did so well we barely noticed, was to nudge us toward writing what was important to us and not trying to please him or anyone else whose approval we craved. Robert Frost said, "No tears in the writer, no tears in the reader. No surprise in the writer, no surprise in the reader." What I learned from Ted, though he never explicitly said so, was *no import for the writer, no import for the reader*.

At the end of our hour, as I gathered my things, Ted lifted his pen above his own poem and crossed out the lines showing his old dog Howard pacing around the bottom of the ladder and trying to climb partway up. "It's too much," he said.

Maybe it was. Maybe it wasn't. But I finally had a better idea of what Ted liked, and it turns out what Ted likes has nothing to do with what Ted likes.

1,001 Things to Amend Before You Die—
Excerpt 244–258

AGE NINE

244. Losing the quartz rock your oldest brother gave you to start your own collection
245. Congratulating your brother instead of admitting you didn't know what it meant when he said he'd been laid off from Boeing
246. Your rush of relief when you realized your parents hadn't called you downstairs to yell at you for jumping on the sofa
247. Realizing that while you'd been shouting and jumping on the sofa your parents were figuring out how to tell you your brother, their eldest son, had just died from a seizure in his sleep
248. Not hugging your father as he trembled, swallowed back the impending landslide, then told you your brother was in God's hands now
249. Letting your new best friend borrow your brother's portfolio of sketches
250. Not tracking down your former new best friend when she moved away a few weeks later
251. Scarfing handfuls of chocolates, Cap'n Crunch, and potato chips for dinner while both your parents lay bedridden with pneumonia the following winter
252. Keeping, then not keeping, your mother's secret when she told you, decades later, that your brother's death may have been a suicide—relief from the constant storm of seizures

253. Believing somehow that your misplaced congratulations had contributed to his sense of isolation and that you were partially responsible for his death
254. Deluding yourself into thinking his soul goes with you everywhere
255. Pretending you see his face in every rock
256. Your inability to see his face in every rock
257. Knowing his absence has become a bigger presence in your life than your handful of thread-worn memories
258. Being unable to distinguish between missing him and the pang conjured each time you think of missing him

Ted Is Writing This Morning

Early, pen and ink, in a room of art and books,
dog at his feet, Buddy or one of the others,
warm heart of the dog necessary to the work.
A walk later, but first, metaphor.
Ted is writing, polishing the poem
like a stone in his hand, turning it over
in his palm. It's smooth now, ready,
so he rises. The sun's up. Buddy's there
or the ghost of some other dog, maybe Alice
or Howard, dancing in canine eagerness,
legs strong, eyes shining, watching as
Ted gets into his jacket, the dog ecstatic
in circles. Sound of the screen door opening.
Perhaps it's winter's first snow, untracked,
or it's a morning in April, the pear tree
fragrant with blossom. The pond smooth as sky,
white ducks moving on it with barely a wake.
The man with the poem walks now to
the water's edge. He draws his arm back.
The heft, the pleasing weight of it—
there will be ripple after ripple. The poem
leaves his hand and arcs out over the water.

. . .

Ted's dogs show up in my poem. I got to know and appreciate
his dogs over the years, especially while being the dog sitter at
one point when Ted and Kathleen had gone on a trip. Ted once
gave me one of the wonderful pens he uses. I loved having that,
but it didn't "take," and I went back to writing with my cheapie

pens. His practice of writing early every morning, though, that "took." The before-sunrise habit fits into my life; I write early before the day gets away from me. I thank Ted for his example in that, as in so many other important poetry practices.

From Description to Discovery

That first day in his office, we didn't talk about poetry. Ted gestured at the armchair neighboring his. And, when I sat down, it seemed only natural to mention the painting on the facing wall—a still life, if I remember correctly, which gleamed with antique darkness—and to talk then of how I had been raised in a household where people often joked, a little seriously, that there was nothing worse than a bare wall.

The room was narrow and quiet. Somehow, it felt protected from the many voices echoing through the main corridor. Much like his poems, Ted's office wasn't fancy but full of useful, appealing objects, the sturdy chairs in one corner, the desk, the bookshelves.

We talked about art. I wanted to make a good impression, wanted to sound as wise as the poems he wrote. If only I could describe, for instance, the way he does in a poem, a box of pastels once owned by the artist Mary Cassatt, some of the pigmented sticks "worn down to stubs" and others "scarcely touched." And, then, as is often the way in Ted's poems, the leap from description to discovery: "I touched / the warm dust of her colors, her tools, / and left there with light on the tips of my fingers."

At some point in our conversation, Ted must have asked me, "Have you gone to the Sheldon yet?" When I shook my head, he nodded for me to take my coat.

And soon we were standing outside the university's art museum, its façade a series of high arches, long stretches of cream-colored marble both classical and modern. Inside, the high ceilings gleamed with enormous, gilded circles, like the heads of huge flowers. Glass. Metal. More stone everywhere.

As we walked through the exhibits, Ted pointed to various pieces, talked about them as if he were discussing old friends—

this canvas so welcoming, that one a little standoffish at first but generous, once you got to know it. It was important, he explained, to really see what one saw. We came to the room that held one of the Sheldon's most famous paintings, Edward Hopper's *Room in New York*, from 1932. We sat on a bench before it.

A man and woman have been placed in the rectangular boundaries of a small room. He's hunched forward in a red armchair, a newspaper in his hands. She has turned her body away from him, her finger resting on one of the white keys of an upright piano. A small round table stands between them and a tall door to another room. He's still wearing his clothes from work—is he a banker or an accountant? She's in a red dress, sleeveless and long, some kind of frill barely visible at her shoulder. Perhaps, they were supposed to go out for dinner and a concert. But he has changed his mind. Now they aren't speaking, and the room contains what each one refuses to say to the other. He reads or pretends to read. She doesn't touch the musical instrument hard enough to make a sound. And we, the viewers, are watching them from outside a large window that frames the scene. We must be waiting in the night, because the ledge is in shadow, and the room is the bright yellow of artificial light.

All these years later, I understand why Ted showed me *Room in New York*. "There's a story here," he had told me. There was a story, I saw, for anyone who knew how to read the thoughtful arrangement of objects: the shape of the man's indifference, the woman still in her boredom or weariness or anger, and the room capable of containing their silence forever.

Reading my own poem, I can see Ted's influence in every line. The extended metaphor. The ordinary objects laid out across the page to tell the story of a marriage. And in the closing lines, I see the same lift toward the lyrical. I recall how Ted describes a box of pastels—the brightness of those dusty colors smeared on fingertips—and so my own poem ends with the shimmering light of the rain.

Pledge

Now we are here at home in the little nation
of our marriage, swearing allegiance to the table
we set for lunch or the windchime on the porch,

its easy dissonance. Even in our shared country,
the afternoon allots its golden lines
so that we're seated, both in shadow, on opposite

ends of a couch and two gray dogs between us.
There are acres of opinions in this house.
I make two cups of tea, two bowls of soup,

divide an apple equally. If I were a patriot,
I would call the blanket we spread across our bed
the only flag—some nights we've burned it

with our anger at each other. Some nights
we've welcomed the weight, a woolen scratch
on both our skins. My love, I am pledging

to this republic, for however long we stand,
I'll watch with you the rain's arrival in our yard.
We'll lift our faces, together, toward the glistening.

A Toast to Chance, Good Fortune, and Ted Kooser

Wildflowers bloomed along NE–80D on the way into Garland. I followed Ted's directions, passed the Germantown Bank, continued over the railroad tracks and by the grain elevator, then followed the curve of the gravel road. Public power workers wearing hard hats and plaid shirts leaned like woodpeckers from utility poles. Over another hill, the red metal gate stood open in welcome. A short lane led into a circular drive. Small red buildings formed an irregular arc beyond.

The house, "an old farmstead sheltered among trees in a valley," as Ted describes it in *Local Wonders*, was gray with crisp white trim. A narrow brick walkway led to the door. Two big dogs, lean and friendly and well behaved, greeted me when Ted opened the screen. His beard, so vivid in my memory, had been lost to radiation therapy.

Ted welcomed me into his home, and Hattie and Buddy joined us in the living room where they dozed. "I've been working on a poem this morning," Ted began. His index finger held his place in the sketch book. "It's my father's birthday. He'd be ninety-seven today. Do you want to hear it?"

Of course I did. It had taken me three decades and 1,500 miles to get here.

Poetry came into my life by chance and Ted's poetry by good fortune. When a playwriting class at New York University was cancelled, I transferred to poetry writing with Bill Packard, editor of the *New York Quarterly*. When Bill, a friend of Karl Shapiro—with whom Ted had studied—learned I was from Nebraska, he brought in a mimeographed sheaf of Ted's early poems that took me back home and welcomed me to the world of Nebraska poetry.

Years later, when I began graduate work at the University of Nebraska–Omaha, *Weather Central* appeared on Dr. Susan Maher's syllabus for Seminar in Plains Literature. When Danielle Glaszner, a fellow classmate, and I teamed up to lead a class discussion on Ted's book, we discovered that little critical attention had been paid to his poetry. We wrote the poet requesting an interview. Ted, then vice president of public relations for an insurance company, called with an alternative: "I'm driving to Omaha for a business meeting. I could stay on to speak to your class. Would that work?" We couldn't imagine anything better.

After his visit, we kept in touch by email. When I moved to Lincoln, he was the first poet I interviewed when I began my dissertation research on contemporary Nebraska poetry. I was fortunate to be a member of Ted's first poetry tutorial.

Later, when I was at work on *The Life and Poetry of Ted Kooser*, Ted welcomed questions and shared photo albums, journals, and newspaper clippings. On trips to his studio in Dwight ("Poetry Made and Repaired Here"), he welcomed my kids, too, showing them to the old tree out back to climb while we talked. We always ended up at Cy's for lunch.

A research highlight was an afternoon with Ted in Guttenberg located in the hills of the upper Mississippi Valley. The little town did not seem to have changed much since Ted described it in "Lights on a Ground of Darkness." We met on Front Street and crossed to the shady riverbank. The breeze still carried the smell of fish and the sound of gulls. Behind us were the limestone buildings that German and Swiss immigrants built in the mid-1800s. The old button factory, now a guesthouse, did not look much different than it did in old postcards.

Ted gave me a tour of the countryside along Jolly Ridge Road. Heading back into Guttenberg, he pulled off into the Mississippi Valley Lookout Point, the center of calm that he imagined during chemo treatments. Our last stop was his grandparents' bungalow, alongside what had been the family's Standard Oil station, now a nursery and bait shop. Ted introduced me to his cousin, the proprietor, who invited us to look around the house. "They enclosed the porch," he said as we approached, and I thought of the boy on the swing during the evenings, listening to the murmur of voices as the grownups played pinochle.

A few days later Ted sent me "House by the Road," commemorating our visit to the little house, "where Liz Moser's lean white chickens / stepped with such purpose over the lawn" and now "a fleet of wet pallets with seedlings / nodding in flats is lashed by green hoses / to the dock of the present."

More years have passed, and more miles traveled. My good fortune continues. Like life's traveler that Ted describes in *Local Wonders*, I lift my glass, to Ted and to the "world, colorful as flying leaves" that he has given us.

Ted Kooser's Near South History Tour

The day Ted gave me a ride to my house, there was a storm, one of those Nebraska spring thunderstorms with staccato lightning. Ted and I had just finished teaching. We were in the mail room commenting on our classes, as well as the booming thunder outside. The way I remember it: After another flicker of lightning, I told Ted I had ridden my bike to school that morning without paying attention to weather reports, but now riding back would not be such a good idea. Ted asked me where I lived. "The Near South on C Street," I said. He immediately offered me a ride since he was headed in that direction.

"I lived here in the city and in the Near South for many years," he told me as we began our short drive. Soon we were on what I now call "Ted's Near South History Tour."

Ted explained how he first lived in an apartment on A Street. He was a graduate student then and newly married. They didn't stay there long and soon moved from A to a duplex on R street. That duplex is the setting for his essay, "Small Rooms in Time." I didn't read his essay until long after this day where I could feel the care in his words as he described these places we were visiting. In the essay he writes: "I began to think about the way in which the rooms we inhabit, if only for a time, become unchanging places within us, complete in detail."

The writer Lee Martin wrote about Ted's essay in "Nostalgia and the Memoirist," noting how Ted resists nostalgia in the essay by writing with an "unflinching eye," unafraid to reveal the disappointments, the sadness, the imperfections that place can evoke. But on our drive that day, Ted was jovial, happily telling me about his son's birth during that time on A Street. After that, they moved to Garfield, but soon the marriage ended. That's when he moved to an apartment on C Street, not far from my house. He lived there for six years before buying a house on Washington.

A few minutes later, we stopped in front of the house on Washington. Ted pointed to the eaves under the porch. He explained how he had painted bright-colored flowers there. He seemed very fond of this memory, how he had decided to decorate the house with his art. Yet, in the downpour, we couldn't see the flowers, and Ted wondered if maybe the owners had painted over them. He went on to tell me that he married his second wife while they lived there, and seven years later, they moved to the house in the country where they are now. We had a talk about the task of making a house one's own, about painting murals on house walls, and painting landscapes in oils and watercolors.

When we arrived at my house, I invited Ted inside. The storm had not quite let up. We ran inside, and I was proud to show him how my partner and I had remodeled the living room and kitchen of this 1917 home, a house where at one time a family of five lived. He quietly scanned the room and then stared at the French doors that led to the backyard deck. By this time, the wind was up, and the rain was hitting the glass doors and windows horizontally. Ted kept staring outside, walking closer to the French doors.

I thought: What is he looking at?

He looked back at me and said, "Did you ever notice the way rain falls on glass?"

He pressed his finger against the glass, following the raindrops, now like tiny rivulets of water zigzagging down the glass door.

"Rain never falls down the glass," he said. "It doesn't move like you might expect. It follows the shape and curve of the pane."

His finger continued to move slowly down. His enthusiasm was not just earnest. I took it as a reminder to clearly look and that looking is the most important task of the artist. Did you ever notice? Did you see? Are you watching? Ted's work is a deep and passionate awareness. That moment: Ted following the raindrop's trail with his finger on the French door was the culmination of that day's lesson from "Ted's Near South History Tour."

And when I think of his work, his poetry and prose, I think of antique cupboards in a kitchen opened and closed by tired hands, paint chipping, cracked boards, a faded tattoo: objects and individuals whose movements and memories tell of the human condition, of mistakes made, regrets, and also of beauty, of love. His awareness of home and belonging is palpable, and for me, a Los Angeles, California, native, he's helped me see and appreciate Nebraska's beauty. Ted, the following poem, "Platte River," which you edited more than once, is dedicated to you.

Platte River

Flat water
When I cross the Nebraska state line
you wind round this land:
bluestem, bluegrass, buffalo grass lands
the gramas and Indiangrass,
that long prairie cordgrass.

You run beside me at Sidney,
past Ogallala and Sutherland,
look dry and tired under the bridges
at Gothenburg and Cozad
but continue to feed the soybean,
the alfalfa fields past Lexington.

So many cars pass you on I–80,
ebony asphalt newly laid, white lines inflexible
against your continual bending course
near the confluence of truck stops, construction corridors.
"I'm traveling in some vehicle," Joni sings,
"Orbiting around the sun."

At Kearney, one great egret
unfolds its wings from your riparian strip.
Long black legs trail behind
while just a quarter mile later,
farmers on their balers spit out
their hay in round fat chunks.

I gas up near the Wood River Motel,
same time a Harley women's club roars in.
River patches on leather chaps,

turquoise side-laced tees and studded boots.
Cool spangled braids stream down their backs,
water reflecting off their shades.

We're on the edge,
the very tip of Sandhill Crane habitat, your tributary,
dotted with blinds to watch them dance in the early spring,
how they circle and land on you at dusk.
These sandhill mounds down the middle of your back
are vacant now, look muted against the verdant green of
    summer.

You shape like a snake, flat water,
almost coiled like Coatlalopeuh
your distant cousin,
reminding me from where I come
and where I'm going
taking you with me always.

ANDREA HOLLANDER

The Things Themselves

Karl Shapiro once defined poetry not as a way of saying things but as a way of seeing them. I thought about this one late February afternoon in 1980 when I first read some of Ted Kooser's poems in a review by Peter Stitt in the *Georgia Review*. I'd dragged a kitchen chair into the miniscule yard of the two-family rental in eastern Texas where we lived while my husband planted pine seedlings for a paper company. This was our first warm day there, and our two-year-old son was anxious to spend it outdoors.

I don't remember what Peter Stitt said about Kooser's book, *Sure Signs*. What struck me were the poems themselves. Stitt had graciously presented whole poems instead of fragments, perhaps a half-dozen of them, each memorable in its way of delivering some small aspect of the world and rendering it brighter and more significant. And more alive.

I still remember the six lines of "Snow Fence," which I recited to my son many winters later when we passed just such a fence on a driving trip to Colorado:

The red fence
takes the cold trail
north; no meat
on its ribs,
but neither has it
much to carry.

Animateness is what continues to strike me about Kooser's way of seeing. He is a master of metaphor in all its incarnations (simile, personification, analogy), but never does his language seem forced or pasted on. Instead his images rise from the things themselves and thus have the feel of authenticity. Here is "Birthday," another poem from *Sure Signs*:

> Somebody deep in my bones
> is lacing his shoes with a hook.
> It's an hour before dawn
> in that nursing home.
> There is nothing to do but get dressed
> and sit in the darkness.
> Up the hall, in the brightly lit skull,
> the young pastor is writing his poem.

One way to demonstrate Kooser's distinctiveness is the way the moon, too often tritely rendered in the poems of so many other poets, finds its place in his work: "my life is a moon / in the frail blue branches / of my veins" ("August"); "At two in the morning, when the moon / has driven away, / leaving the faint taillight of one star / at the horizon" ("Highway 30"); "I sometimes / take hold of the cold porcelain knob / of the moon, and turn it, and step into a room" ("November 12").

Winter Morning Walks: One Hundred Postcards to Jim Harrison, written during the poet's recuperation and recovery from cancer, is one of Kooser's most powerful collections. Each of its brief poems was written after a predawn walk and begins with a date and brief weather report. Any one of the poems will exhibit Kooser's ability to distinguish the animate within the inanimate. Here is "December 14," its epigram, "Home from my walk, shoes off, at peace":

> The weight of my old dog, Hattie—thirty-five pounds
> of knocking bones, sighs, tremors and dreams—
> just isn't enough to hold a patch of sun in its place,
> at least for very long. While she shakes in her sleep,

it slips from beneath her and inches away,
taking the morning with it—the music from the radio,
the tea from my cup, the drowsy yellow hours—
picking up dust and dog hair as it goes.

Ten years after reading Peter Stitt's review, I attended my first
national writers' conference because Ted Kooser was on the
faculty. As suspected, he was a fine teacher—filled with wise,
practical advice, lots of good feeling and humor, and no academic
jargon. At another writers' conference, one that I directed five
years later, he explained why he included in some of his poems
the whole names of people no general reader will have heard
of—Ira Friedlein, Nels Paulssen, Joe Skala, and Todd Halle, to
name a few. It's a way to honor someone, to keep his memory
alive, Kooser said.

Even when the honoree is someone famous, Kooser manages
to celebrate his or her personhood, as in "A Box of Pastels,"
for example, from the poet's most recent collection, *Delights &*
Shadows:

I once held on my knees a simple wooden box
in which a rainbow lay dusty and broken.
It was a set of pastels that had years before
belonged to the painter Mary Cassatt,
and all of the colors she'd used in her work
lay open before me. Those hues she'd most used,
the peaches and pinks, were worn down to stubs,
while the cool colors—violet, ultramarine—
had been set, scarcely touched, to one side.
She'd had little patience with darkness, and her heart
held only a measure of shadow. I touched
the warm dust of those colors, her tools,
and left there with light on the tips of my fingers.

I now own every book Kooser has published, and I've purchased issues of literary journals just because they contain his work. My son, too, now twenty-seven, has become a lover of poetry. Ted Kooser is greatly to blame.

Old Snow

After the eponymous 1999 oil painting by Ted Kooser
and his poetry collection *Winter Morning Walks*

Between the pasture
and the old quarry road,
it snakes for acres
along the fencerow.
It refuses to give in
to the early morning sun,
only a hint in the distance.
To escape the bitter wind,
a few cows gather
behind a sagging barn
unseen in the painting.
But the painter himself
has walked this fence line
all winter long, leaving
his house before dawn,
the fur-lined flaps of his cap
muffling the sounds
of bellowing cows
or an occasional farm truck
rattling to a start in the cold.
This early, the first light
is only a suggestion
suggesting the landscape.
But the man follows
the pale white line
and the world grows
more and more visible.

He tries not to think
of the cancer now
months behind him.
At the mile marker
he turns back. All that's left
of the storm is this single
meandering drift, a roll
of weathered gauze
weary from being wound
and unwound, now flung out
beside this barbed wire fence,
the man who once needed it
walking without it toward home.

STEPHEN BEHRENDT

The Surprising Novelty of the Familiar:
Ted Kooser's Poetry

Ezra Pound told his modernist contemporaries, about a century ago, to "make it new!" But it was *his* predecessor—by a full century—who explained why they should do so and then demonstrated how to do it. Writing about the poems he had contributed to his and his friend Coleridge's collaborative collection, *Lyrical Ballads*, William Wordsworth explained his decision to "choose incidents and situations from common life" and to describe them in "language really used by men [*and women*, I'll add here]." At the same time, he hoped to "throw over them a certain coloring of imagination, whereby ordinary things should be presented to the mind in an unusual way" in order to "make these incidents and situations interesting" by correlating them with "the primary laws of our nature." The goal was nothing less than to rescue the ordinary from the indifference bred of familiarity, to raise it from humility to transcendence, to dignify—indeed to sanctify—the quotidian, the everyday, the unappreciated wealth that surrounds us.

Over my years as both a poet and a teacher I've often found myself thinking about how very right Wordsworth was when it comes to poetry's role in the public culture, and about his efforts to make his own poetry approachable for the "ordinary" reader. Partly this is because the things that I write about in my own poems tend to come from that everyday world, a world accessible to each of us, no matter our location or circumstances. And like Wordsworth, I'm interested in alerting what is usually called the "general reader" to the exceptional that resides in the everyday. Poetry is an inherently democratizing art, after all, not an effete one; as Wordsworth labored to teach us, each of us has the capacity to be a poet too. I've always told my students that his best poems are a hands-on instruction manual (pun intended) that teaches each of us how to *be* that poet, how to see and feel as the poet sees and feels, and how to use the raw materials for doing so that are strewn all around us in the various familiar worlds each of us inhabits.

Like countless readers in America and abroad, I'm a longtime Ted Kooser fan who never tires of his remarkable ability to reveal those wonders of daily life and experience that are so often—so easily—overlooked. So I suppose it is really not surprising that I was reminded again of Wordsworth the first time I read Ted's recent title poem, "Red Stilts" (2020). This lovely little poem epitomizes for me the essence of Ted's poetry and the distinctive, humane poetic that shapes and informs it. It's such a simple thing that Ted describes here, this stilt-making: something that many of us of a certain age will recognize, just as we will relate immediately to the paint-sticky fingers that betray the irresistible eagerness to *use* those newly fashioned stilts. Ted understands what Wordsworth also understood: that the authenticity of any poem's emotional power is rooted in the authenticity of the poem's physical details. And so he gives us the physiology of the stilts, the physical dimensions of the vertical shafts and the specific placement of the foot-blocks, and then that remarkable and seemingly unremarkable old chair on which he recalls placing his new-painted stilts. Just "a saggy, ancient Adirondack chair," he remembers. The physical specificity of "Adirondack" balances the suggestively, impressionistically vague adjectives, "saggy" and "ancient," each disclosing its own softly nuanced nature while also supplementing and subtly modifying the others. Even that's not enough, though, it seems. We need to acknowledge, too, the impossibility of the poor old chair ever living up any more to its intended function ("no longer good for much"—"much" meaning, presumably, sitting in). We're reminded instead of its present inglorious, diminished state: holding gardening implements and bundled plant stakes, these unassuming details leaning on one another, growing into one another, like the invisible pea- and bean-tendrils or tomato vines the stakes imply—and like the poem's bundled adjectives themselves.

It's not just a poem about *stilts*, though, is it? Nor is it just about Ted Kooser the boy "seventy years ago" and the man "now," nor is it just about Kooser the poet and craftsman who ties together those two seventy-years-separated figures from the first and final stanzas through his masterfully subtle wordplay with "block(s)" in those two stanzas. Nor is it, either, just about *all* of us, individually and collectively, recognizing the deep truth of what the poem describes—if not from our own personal experience, then from those comparable experiences we have heard from parents and grandparents whose retellings likewise transcend time and space. Like so many of Ted's poems, "Red Stilts" is also about what we do when we read. Indeed, his insistence on the intellectual, imaginative and spiritual value of that reading activity helps explain Ted's longstanding commitment to his weekly column, American Life in Poetry. In the painfully unpoetic times in which we now live, is there a place, anymore, for poetry, for poets, and for the restorative power of imaginative activity? Ted argues that, yes, there is indeed. My own experience as a poet and as a teacher tells me that he is absolutely right. And his readers agree too.

That reader buy-in is important, too—especially when it comes to poetry—and that's surely another reason why Ted's poetry resonates with readers of widely diverse backgrounds. It's accessible—and that's no easy effect to achieve—trust me. Its source materials are the familiar features of our daily lives; its language is a rich amalgam of what we hear all around us. Put at ease by both Ted's companionable descriptive details and his unostentatious idiom, we forget our habitual anxiety about poetry's supposed "difficulty" and open ourselves up to the unexpected—unsuspected—wonders that reside in the seemingly plain garb. Getting us to do so is the sure sign of a mature poetic craft: by revealing what's hidden in plain sight, Ted teaches us to see, to hear, to "enter into" his subjects. I stress the gentle seductiveness of effective poetry with my students when I teach poetry, and I do my best to practice it in my own writing. It's part of the implied compact that any conscientious writer makes with her or his readers. Because we often read "by ourselves," in relative privacy, we tend to forget that reading is in fact an act of community: when we read, we join the poet in a process of co-creation in which we "complete"—by "performing" it as a reader—the work that the poet has *begun*. Reading enacts an imaginative consciousness expansion through which we both perceive *and participate in* the organic universal community of which we are all members. That world, we may suddenly realize, is not some "mere" aggregation of inanimate objects but, rather, a vibrant, *living* universe. Not just people, but also *things* are alive: they have lives; they have *life*. And so do we.

My poems tend to focus on the "things" of the everyday world, too, because we too easily forget about the "lives" that such things contain. I wrote a poem called "Coyote" some years ago, after we had moved into a semirural outskirt of Lincoln where coyotes ran free, had their pups in copses and coverts and cornfields and sang in the fields in the night. In my poem one such gorgeous beast crosses into the wrong field, is felled by two gunshots and dies amid the field flowers. It was important to me that those plants be *real*—not just some generic collection of "weeds." And so I called them by their names: spiderwort and mullein and sage, just as I described the coyote's butter-colored fur and ragged ear. The truth of any poem depends on the authenticity of its details, its explicit ties to the factuality of the physical world. It's important for the poet to know, for example, that the ubiquitous wildflower *Linaria vulgaris* (or common toadflax) is sometimes called "butter-and-eggs" by farm women because of the color of its blossoms, and "rabbit flower" by their husbands because of its invasive spread. Even if the poet never shares that information explicitly with the reader, it's something that the poet nevertheless needs to know. Such knowledge is evocative and revelatory in the way that the French word for potatoes—*pommes de terre*—means "apples of the earth." It opens up new and unanticipated vistas. It stimulates the imagination. This is why the authenticity of Ted's "Red Stilts" is rooted in particularizing details like the fact that the red paint on the "six-foot two-by-twos" is *still tacky*. It's the little things. Another Romantic poet, William Blake, reminded us to "Labor well the minute Particulars" because they are the "outward expressions in this world of the eternal individualities of all things." And there's that word *things* again, hand in hand with eternal individuality and "life" that is not hemmed in by time, place, or circumstance—and yet firmly rooted in the familiar, the commonplace, the everyday.

For me, it's only a short and natural step from that Romantic conviction about the life that dwells in *things* to Ted Kooser's stilts. Not just mere "things," they, too, contain *life itself*. Indeed, they *are* life. And so when we read this or so many other of Ted's poems, we join a community of heightened imaginative activity and co-create with him the poem *and all it holds and communicates*. That's the nature of the transcendent experience: it alters our consciousness and expands our capacity to imagine, to create, to participate in something larger, greater than ourselves. Poetry has the singular capacity to make us all equal—if only we will allow ourselves to be so—by virtue of the imagination's power to transform the ordinary. Seeing—really *seeing*—the extraordinary in the everyday realities that lie all around us and that we habitually take so unresponsively for granted: that's the key. It's what guides me in my writing, no less than in my teaching—something else I'm happy to believe I share with Ted. The best art reminds us of that restorative potential, again and again. How many of us have traveled far and wide to admire some fabled beauty, having in the meantime failed to recognize those beauties that hide in plain sight in our own backyards? So it is in poetry, too. And it's why so many diverse readers have discovered in those weekly newspaper columns, where Ted introduces poets writing across America, voices that speak to them of familiar things. My students are often intimidated by poetry because it has so often been presented to them as a sort of intellectual hocus-pocus, something rarified, elitist, and imaginatively off-putting. It doesn't need to be that way, Ted's poems remind us. We should pay attention, listen, relax, and recognize ourselves there in what we contemplate.

Among the many features I so admire in the poetry of my long-time colleague and friend Ted Kooser is his lifelong commitment to showing us the transformational wonders of those ordinary "things" that so many of us routinely pass by without notice or comment, those wonders that await us all if only we will pause to "see into" them. Whether it's paper cones of "sticky, spun sweetness" at the fair ("Cotton Candy," 2020), or the wingtips of soaring dark birds "fanned like fingertips" ("Turkey Vultures," 2003), or the old gravel road, "its billow of dust / full of the sparks of redwing blackbirds" ("So This Is Nebraska," 1980), or the bird chirping in the early morning rain "its sweet-sour / wooden-pulley notes" ("The Early Bird," 2003), these "small wonders" are the hallmarks of Ted Kooser's unfailingly eloquent, accessible poems. Like "the bedroom wall / papered with lilacs and the kitchen shelves / covered with oilcloth" ("Abandoned Farmhouse," 1980), they are the achingly authentic details that assure us of the transformative reality that his poetry gently teaches. All this he does in "the language really used" by "real" people. I'm flattered that Ted has invited me—invited *us*—to join him in the act of creating and completing this work that he has so well begun for so many years. And I'm grateful—very grateful—for that generous gift.

Supper with Amy

She sets the table and tells me
There's nothing better
than sharing a whole roasted chicken

with someone you love.
Still learning how to be
in each other's company,

we are polite, slice our meat
with a knife. But when she says

I've devoured a whole chicken
using nothing but my hands,
something about the picture

of her pulling apart a wing with her teeth,
her fingers shimmering in grease,
makes me confess,

I am so lonely. Later,
the moon rises slow and low

as she strokes the arch of my foot with her thumb,
telling me that the one man
whose sweat she lived to smell and taste

was the same one who, after years,
she could not let enter
her house. I imagine them on her porch,
both leaning in
even as she warns,

Your lips better not brush my neck.

Sated, Amy and I sit in the almost-dark
and let it reach us like breath—

the toothsome memory
of coming undone,
our bodies starved, wrecked.

. . .

Ted's poems have always shown us how the smallest conversations, objects, and happenings in our everyday lives are infused with incredibly complex stories. "Supper with Amy" reflects how Ted's sensibility has impacted my work and my worldview. Like Kooser's "Abandoned Farmhouse," "In The Basement of the Goodwill Store," and "A Room in the Past," I hope to write poems that illuminate all the ways in which, as Ted promised in his wonderful book *The Poetry Home Repair Manual,* "The large is present in the small."

MARK SANDERS

A Summer Letter to Old Friends Up North

Late-July, and rain has come and gone
and come again, driving down the farm road
and over pasture fences in black Mack trucks;
the back gates fly open, and out leap the bulls
that piss and thunder on mighty hooves. *Humidity*
is like calling the Gulf a bead of sweat.
Meanwhile, the boating here is good, on top this hill,
where in the distance I can see the haze
blue as tsunami. The cattle, across that stretch,
have drowned, it seems, the oak ridge submerged
like a submarine. A few hummingbirds remain, poor things,
though they're likely confused: the tropics
came north with them, and they must believe
they've missed the winter. I watch them weave
an invisible web among the bottlebrush
and esperanza. I can but wonder what they'll net
besides my hope. Toads, as big as sandbags
too heavy to carry, honk in the fields,
and herons and egrets, starving, circle overhead.
Thus are the tidings from Texas: waves of fire ants
and ticks, copperheads and cottonmouths.
It's been two years or more since I've seen you last.
I wish you well—and cold and snow and ice,
the closest to which I have in hand a frozen margarita,
tart enough and salty to cut the bite of tequila.
I sit sipping on the porch in my wooden rocker,
next to a wicker table where a candle burns
to deter mosquitoes, some as big as poodles.
In this heat wax melts fast, though for now the wick stays lit.
If I noodle a catfish, I will have to send a picture.

. . .

"A Summer Letter to Old Friends Up North" takes its lead from Ted's "A Dry Winter Letter to Friends," from *Not Coming to Be Barked At* (1976). I took a departure from Ted's seriousness, however, and, because I live in Texas (where everything is *big*), exaggeration was in order.

SHARON CHMIELARZ

Aunt Bertha

In autumn the summerhouse door she shoved
open landed her in a stuffy room, soon to
swarm in sugar steam from scalded jars:
the annual canning, *putting up*—Aunt Bertha
heating up the canner's water on the old stove.

On August's agenda—crab apples. Hers from
trees not grafted to bear miniature inedibles
but troves of reds and yellows guarded from
bird pillage and savored as *the* ingredient
for sauce when a woman lives in the same place

all her life. Like her you'd notice, too, the fields
getting so they were all lakes and marshes.
You'd be happy, too, when women could wear
pants on the tractor or at work with the header.
"That was *hardt*," Aunt Bertha huffed, "in a dress."

When company stopped by she served sauce.
Crabapple sauce. With a square of cake.
Like her mother. And now her daughter-in-law.
The apple, says the proverb, doesn't fall far
Der Apfel fällt nicht weit . . . from the tree.

. . .

I love the way Ted Kooser records midwestern women of a certain
age. I chose "Aunt Bertha" for this volume because it's a bit of a
companion to his "Applesauce" (*Delights & Shadows*).

Sustenance

Summer, 2020, and though I've moved back to my hometown of Seward, Nebraska, I can't visit my friend, Ted Kooser. The pandemic has sent him into a poet's hibernation in the refuge of his Bohemian Alps, though Ted has found ways to welcome me. My first week in town, he asked if I wouldn't like to have the century-old piano that lived in his studio in Dwight, as I'd played it for him anytime I was in town to visit. My second week here, he decided he could part with the phonograph and stereo he'd used at Dwight, and even with some records. It was the third week, when he arrived unannounced to my driveway in his red truck, overalls, and mask, that I realized my summer would be marked by Ted's unmatchable generosity, as I watched him unload a bicycle from the bed of the truck. When Ted loves you, he wishes you to thrive—the same wish he has for the world and every speck of nature, or even waste, within it (who else has published such moving words about a littered plastic bag?).

This year marks our fifth as friends, though when I lost an uncle last year, Ted offered to become my uncle, if I'd like. I did like. I love, in fact. Before he was my uncle, Ted's poems, with their moments of both piercing light and shadowed grief, sustained me as I walked into early and middle adult life, from a childhood in Nebraska to decades beyond in places like New York, Texas, and India. As I came to writing seriously in my thirties, I couldn't put pen to paper without an invocation of at least one Kooser poem. Soon I'd find myself procrastinating my own work, as I'd become engulfed in the screech owls, boxelder bugs, and soft hands of Ted's elderly relatives. Whether wind or widow, opossum or old maid, Ted's characters all felt like mine. And so one gray February morning, over five years ago, I broke the seal and wrote Ted a letter. Thankfully, he replied. We've been friends, and now family, ever since.

February 18, 2015

Dear Mr. Kooser,

My name is Suzanne Ohlmann and I'm writing to you today from San Antonio, Texas, though I am not a Texan. I live here with my husband, Ryan Westerhoff, both of us Seward, Nebraska, kids, both of us having found each other after years apart and miles away from the Garland hills.

We're happy here in San Antonio, with an old house, a front porch, and a century-old ash tree in the yard. Ryan works as a firefighter at the station down the block. I stay home and work as a nurse investigator, deciphering medical stories gone wrong and whether or not the attorneys who pay me should pursue a case.

We are exiled Nebraskans, and we've come to rely on your writing as more than inspiration, or a gateway to nostalgia, but as sustenance. I grew up in a literary house, the tall brick one on the corner of 5th and Hillcrest, the place often mistaken for the parsonage of the Episcopal church. My mom a teacher, my dad a librarian at Concordia, books, language and literature were the idiom of the Ohlmann house. (My mom sends me your new books as soon as they are published, and Ryan and I lie on our backs and recite the new poems to each other. Ryan still can't read "Painting the Barn" without a moment to collect himself. Even those first three words catch in his throat: *My good dog, Alice . . .*)

But Ryan grew up on a farm east of town, a country boy, an athlete, not a book on a shelf, not a moment spent hearing his father read or his mother run off to book club. He appreciates the idea of literature, but until we reunited several years ago, he didn't live with books.

And until my life brought me back to Ryan, and thus back to Nebraska (in Texas, of all places), I didn't read or hear your work the way I do now. Ryan and I knew and loved old women like your mother's cousin, Pearl. We drank instant coffee at the kitchen tables of our grandparents. We visited my grandpa's abandoned farmhouse northeast of Columbus and found his old, cast-iron truck toy in a pile of leaves under the back porch and took it with us all the way home to Texas. We cleaned it with mineral oil and brought back some of the old red paint, and just a little bit of Grandpa, too.

We feel lucky to walk our dogs through the neighborhood and pass houses with signs in the yard that read, "*We Don't Dial 911!*" and, "*Come and Take It!*" and breathe and know that when we get home, we can take out our copy of *Delights & Shadows* and open up to any poem, say, "Memory," and in a matter of minutes, we, too, are bound up in the winds of that tornado, sitting at that table of chicken and ham and mashed potatoes (and peas, my grandma's favorite, though she served all her vegetables creamed).

When I'm not doing my law job, I write, and work now digging up my own story from under the back porch of an otherwise healthy, stable childhood and life. I was born in Grand Island and adopted nine days later into my Seward family. I've stumbled into a good deal of grief along the way, a lot of vertical space amidst the flat, wide terrain of the Platte. My hope is to come to a place where the story captures both, and with as few, well-honed words as possible.

This is why I appreciate your work. This is why I start my writing with reading one of your poems aloud. This is why I read "Pearl" as part of my Oral Interpretation class at my Master of Fine Arts program at Wilkes University in Wilkes-Barre, Pennsylvania.

After I read "Pearl," several of my fellow students approached me after to ask your name, titles of books, etc.

"Ted Kooser," I said to them.

"Coosher?" they asked.

"Koo-zer," I said.

"Hoosier?" they asked.

I finally just wrote it down.

They meant well, and I hope they bought some books.

Ryan and I will come home to Nebraska in March. I've never seen the cranes. I was born at the height of their Platte stopover, on March 22nd. I'm hoping to find a way, in the midst of all those wheeling birds, to discover that I was born in the right place, at the right time, in the middle of something much older, much bigger than a single, human birth.

We hope to visit Garland, too, and hunt down some of Ryan's ancestors. His great-great uncle, Johann (John) Westerhoff, was Germantown's first postmaster. We're eager to drive the country roads and visit the old cemetery west of town. Perhaps we'll pass you some afternoon. We'll be sure to raise just an index finger off the steering wheel when we see you.

Very Sincerely,
Suzanne Ohlmann

JAMES DANIELS

The Crucial Lack of Redemption

I quit drinking when it turned into a part-time job.
—Ted Kooser

I studied Spanish for years and years
but never learned to roll my R's. Like an engine
not turning over, slowly wearing the battery
down. This, after it took me eight years
of remedial speech to correct the slurring
of my words. This, before I began to drink
myself into slurring again. Though even
drunk I could not roll, could not flutter
those beautiful syllables. My father
never learned to say I love you
or use a computer or GPS. I've spent
and wasted great quantities of unspared
change considering what is willful
and what cannot be helped and what
cannot be blamed. Lift the hood
and peer under as if something
could be done. Sometimes you just
have to slam that hood back down
and walk away. I'm a pretty good
walker, I've learned, wearing out
multiple pairs of shoes and blues
on city sidewalks rubbing shoulders
against brick for luck. If I tell you
I stopped drinking, that might suggest
a certain redemption, but there's always
that matter of the R's circling

like flocks of black birds in December
that I can never name.

. . .

This poem was inspired by something Ted said many years ago
at a dinner when he was reading in Pittsburgh. I've carried this
quote—the epigraph to the poem—with me as a kind of talisman
during my years of sobriety. Like Ted's writing, it was a clear,
succinct statement that resonated with layers. Ted said it matter-
of-factly—like he does—and he gave me a line that I can and do
say without shame and without going into messy details when
I'm offered a drink by people who don't know me.

SALLY GREEN

Wildflower

for Ted Kooser

So tiny it's a miracle we see it
even once, lavender-white nestled
in patches of moss
where trees make shade
all day. And to find it
again means having to pay
attention to the smallest
landmarks, move with care,
making the merest whisper
of delight so as not to add more weight
to those stems, thin as bones
in a bird's wing, than its name
—*Scouler's Harebell*—already does.

. . .

One of Ted Kooser's most endearing traits as a poet is the scope
of his vision. Very little escapes his attention, whether it's some-
thing in the natural world or a small object on a yard-sale table.
After reading *Winter Morning Walks*, I found my own attention
heightened, so that I began looking more closely at plants I had
once passed with barely a glance, including the subject plant of
this little poem located just up the hill from our hand-built log
home.

SAMUEL GREEN

Feathering

> *But to what*
> *safe place shall any of us return . . . ?*
> —Ted Kooser

You'll have seen them feeding
on gnats & mosquitoes above ponds
& slow-moving, shallow creeks,
Barn Swallows, just like the four
perched on the rail of our county
dock. Two weeks ago they were nestlings
in a dried cup of mud under the eaves
of the post office porch just above
the bay. Now they seem to be taking
turns launching themselves off the sun-
bleached wood to chase the white
curl of a feather, catch & release,
one after the other, their backs
the color of mussel shells catching
light, turning this way & that
with only a slight shift of wing or
forked tail, the others lined up
& watching, never mind how
the weight of my truck makes
the dock beams shudder, or that
they will not return to their nest,
or that things can, at any time,
turn utterly serious.

. . .

Among the many birds Ted Kooser likes to watch are swallows, but he's not the sort of watcher who merely names and moves on. Always there seems to be a voice in his head saying, "Look closer," and he does. The epigraph for this little poem is taken from his own "At Nightfall," where he meditates on how swallows use a single feather to guide themselves back home. His observation and question moved me toward mine, watching swallows at play at the county dock of our small island home.

MARK IRWIN

The smaller house

While building the larger house he lived a very simple life

in the smaller house he'd built before, the house without

water or power, the 12 x 20 ft. house with three windows,

a single bed, chair, the house whose thousand books lined

the walls, including some he'd written in the house, written

by windowlight, or the Coleman lantern charged each day

at the hot springs pool, where he swam those mornings, and now

living in the larger house with every convenience, he missed living in

the smaller house with none, where sometimes he'd lean against

a dusk-window just to finish a line, or where once in the dark he wrote

in pencil a dream on the wall, then went back to sleep, finding

later by phone-light his words like a string in the forest, while a Bible-black

sky still buckled with stars, fading toward morning, where he walked,

ageless, hunched with axe in his sack cloth, into the new light.

. . .

Caravaggio, the great sixteenth-century Italian painter, writes in a
notebook: "In art, there is nothing more difficult than simplicity."
I've always been deeply moved by this reductive principle, especially
the clarity of scene and strict light in Caravaggio's works, and I've
admired this same principle in Kooser's poems—a striving toward

the essence of both action and silence. Good poems, like good houses, allow us "to dwell" in them, as opposed simply "to exist." I'm so thankful for all of Ted's generous and inviting work, words that supply everything you need, but no more.

Translating Ted Kooser

Before I began the doctoral program at the University of Nebraska, I only knew Ted Kooser as a poem on a page. I had read *Delights & Shadows*, so I knew his concision with words, his strong sense of sound, his ability to transform a seemingly simple moment into profound insight into human interactions, but I had never really explored the man behind the poems. What came next when I signed on for the first time for his tutorial (yes, I took it multiple times), what happened when I sat down in that small office where he kept some of his paintings and sketches, was a life education, not just a poetic one.

In the years that I worked with Ted one-on-one, I read many more of his books of poetry, his prose, an early manuscript of his *Kindest Regards*, and I even had the honor of working through and commenting on a forthcoming manuscript. I found in each the same aspects that he emphasized in our sessions: those very specific observations that transformed writing into an experienced moment that he called the "authenticating detail"; real-world interactions and observations that could be as simple as discovering an old milk jug floating in a pond and that stayed in a specific concrete moment but left you feeling changed; a delightful ear for sound that often made him smile when he heard it in his students' work. Ted could read a student's poem twice and immediately find the weak points that held the poem back. In examining our writing, Ted was no-nonsense. He didn't put up with intellectual flourish; he got rid of unnecessary philosophizing, of pretentious artifice, of showy contrivances. What was left when he was done was inevitably better, more direct, sensory, and clear.

But what made his tutorial different from many of the other workshops I'd been in were the conversations on both poetry and so many other subjects. On any given day, we might talk about a piece of music, repairing hot rods, fence building, or painting, and maybe even swap a joke or two. These conversations were the stuff poetry is made of, and Ted, as the consummate raconteur, always had a story to tell about the topic that was as visual, as experiential as the poems he writes. I think that's because Ted is truly a student of the world. He carries in his shirt pocket a small notebook and a pencil where he records daily observations, ask questions, reminds himself to check on something that has intrigued him. There's no doubt that those musings become his poems.

For me, what had just been a poem on the page has become a man I admire as a teacher, mentor, and friend. I keep going back to the day I visited his studio in Dwight, a small town in Nebraska just off Highway 66. It felt so much like Ted Kooser: a small unassuming town where this treasure trove of art stood, and I mean that literally. Inside there were walls of vinyl country albums, shelves of books, tubs of paints, canvases drying on the floor, charcoals, drawing pencils, and other sketching materials. We sat in the small sitting area at the front of the studio and talked about our lives by telling stories. That's Ted to me: someone with no artifice but deeply engaged with art; someone who sees the world through stories; someone who has experienced so much of the world and can bring it to life through words.

I worked on "Ferris Wheel" with Ted in his tutorial—first in the fall of 2017 and then again on a revised draft in the fall of 2018.

Ferris Wheel

Where I fall from the sky,

the night is a garish woman decked in lights.

A country love song drifts from the grandstand.
I listen to the siren

screaming in the distance: *we got a winner here.*
            Below me

the funhouse flashing lights, haunted laughter
swallowed by the Horror House doors, the couples

clinging to each other. The Galaxy

whips its octopus arms
throwing children into their screaming faces,

and this wheel keeps dipping into the crowd
like a giant mill. The air is heavy with popcorn

and fry grease, and I can see a carney in the shadows
of a semi, smoking, picking at his face.

Love is not the right word for the way I plunge
Into the metal work arms, lift again

toward that sickle of a moon, seduced
by the simple motion, by a woman

holding a cone of cotton candy who waves
as I pass and licks the sweetness from her fingers.

DANA GIOIA

Discovering Ted Kooser (1980)

In 1980 I came across Ted Kooser's *Sure Signs* in a group of books sent to me for a "Poetry Chronicle" in the *Hudson Review*. Here is, slightly edited, what I wrote. I didn't know this short notice would begin a long personal and professional relationship with the author.

Ever since I lived in Minneapolis, where local connoisseurs informed me in matter-of-fact tones that the Walker Art Gallery was generally acknowledged to rival the Uffizi, the Guthrie summer stock outclassed the Salzburg Festival, the IDS building downtown ranked with Chartres, and Mary Tyler Moore was the new Garbo, I have been suspicious of midwestern cultural boosterism. Therefore, over the past few years when three Nebraskans independently recommended the work of Ted Kooser, a poet who works as an insurance underwriter in Lincoln, I smugly resolved to remain in blissful ignorance. Now confronted with a review copy of *Sure Signs*, a first-rate collection of Kooser's new and selected poems, I abhor my snobbism and repent in dust and ashes. As penance I promise to skip the cartoons in the next five issues of the *New Yorker* and talk for five minutes to the first insurance man who calls during dinner.

Kooser is a master of the short poem. Only two of the eighty-nine poems in *Sure Signs* run longer than one page, and their average length is about a dozen lines. Within these narrow bounds Kooser seems ready to try anything. His poems are most often bizarre, surrealistic anecdotes, little stories where details and metaphors acquire an unruly life of their own. Kooser obsessively sees things as people (ladders as men, mice as refugees, a furnace as an old man), and it is not unusual for one of these things to get up and walk away with the poem. So many of the poems have surprising twists that one never settles into the drowsy half-attention that too much dinner or too much poetry can bring. I found it impossible to put *Sure Signs* down until I had finished the entire book. It was like sitting next to a box of chocolates before dinner. I kept intending to put the book aside to finish later, but kept sneaking one more poem until there were none left. I suspect that praising a book of poems for being so readable will cause suspicion in certain parties. I can only direct the skeptical to the book itself and ask if they can find fault with a collection alternately so delightful and mysterious and always so unassuming.

What is especially refreshing about Kooser's work is the originality of its imagery. Nowadays when most poets plug in "striking, original" images as mechanically as their grandparents plugged in standard rhymes, it is a pleasure to read a poet like Kooser whose imagination is naturally metaphorical. When this gift for metaphor combines with Kooser's eerie sense of humor, the results are usually memorable, as in "Spring Plowing":

West of Omaha the freshly plowed fields
steam in the night like lakes.
The smell of the earth floods over the roads.
The field mice are moving their nests
to the higher ground of fence rows,
the old among them crying out to the owls
to take them all. The paths in the grass
are loud with the squeak of their carts.
They keep their lanterns covered.

Notice how conventionally this surprising poem begins. The first five lines, which could have been written by any competent poet, scarcely prepare us for what follows. Kooser compresses several implicit metaphors into the next four lines before ending with a sinister, enigmatic image. Yet the poem never becomes clumsy or crowded. This macabre smoothness is Kooser's distinctive touch. On the very next page in "Sitting All Evening Alone in the Kitchen" one finds the same smooth, simple surface covering a complex organization of symbols:

The cat has fallen asleep,
the dull book of a dead moth
loose in his paws.

The moon in the window, the tide
gurgling out through the broken shells
in the old refrigerator.

Late, I turn out the lights.
The little towns on top of the stove
glow faintly neon
sad women alone at the bar.

My only complaint is that the book gives no clue to how the poems are organized. Are they arranged chronologically, randomly, or under some organic principle I've not discerned? Still this small confusion cannot hamper the enjoyment of such a unique talent. Learn from my mistakes. Pull down thy vanity and read Ted Kooser.

Old Man in the Hall of Nebraska Wildlife

for Ted Kooser

Elementary school students tumble
into the Hall of Nebraska Wildlife

like elementary school students
who don't want to be here.

A field trip is just a day away from
crayons, math drills, and monkey bars.

They step on the backs of the shoes
of the classmate in front of them

and stare down at a stained carpet
older than their eldest sibling.

They glance up occasionally to see
the animals stiff in their boxed wilderness

until an old man, hunched, sporting
a mesh ball cap from a local gas station

long extinct and a beige Members Only
jacket begins to dart around the hall

like a sidewalk squirrel. His veined hands
press black buttons that bring this tomb to life.

There is the hawk's whistle fade,
the magpie's yips like a machine gun,

the meadowlark with the confident
trill of a soloist who hits the right notes

and nothing more. Before the students
and their chaperones realize it, the man

shoots his arthritic joints down the hall
to summon a growling badger from its den

and the grunts of buffalos in the runt,
which rumble like a jeep powering over

a rocky outcrop. He skips by to push the bird
song buttons again to keep up the cacophony.

The children join in with hums and howls.
They spin like dust devils that soon turn to nothing.

. . .

I dedicated "Old Man in the Hall of Nebraska Wildlife" to Ted
Kooser because he suggested that whenever one visits the Uni-
versity of Nebraska State Museum in Morrill Hall and passes
through the section dedicated to the furs, scales, and feathers
of the Cornhusker State that the only rational thing to do was
to run around the exhibit pressing all the buttons that set off
recorded sounds of bison, prairie rattlers, deer, and numerous
birds. The one time I tried this, I punched a few buttons and
was about to sluggishly dart to the next set when my partner at
the time hissed "Stop it." This pretty much shamed me to let the
noises I had conjured die off. And while the notion of a grown
man galloping around a museum is a silly one, I found the image
irresistible and had to put it down on paper in some way.

Some of my favorite poems by Ted explore abandoned and
rundown spaces, places with a past and weight to them. "The
Red Wing Church" gives the reader a whimsical breakdown of

an old church that has been repurposed and reclaimed by the earthly world. The speaker in "Abandoned Farmhouse" speculates about (and perhaps throws a little bit of shade at) the family who once lived there through the items and junk that remain. It is not surprising that a poet who had a career as an insurance executive would possess a keen eye for details that hint at a person's downfall. I even joked to a few of my fellow graduate students that since Ted had worked in insurance, he probably got a good sense of how long you would live just by looking at you. As I have gotten older, this notion is more haunting than hilarious, but I suppose there is a certain burden that comes from being perceptive.

In August 2009, Lincoln Public Schools named an elementary school in Ted's honor. Where I grew up in Georgia, one usually had to be a former school superintendent, a long-dead slave owner, or die in a horrible car accident in order to get a school named after them. Regional primary-school naming preferences aside, I imagine the students who matriculate through Kooser Elementary at some point take a class field trip to the State Museum and make their way down to the Hall of Nebraska Wildlife to tread across the worn carpet and pass by dioramas devoted to a family of skunks, a dance of sandhill cranes, and a mountain lion chilling on a rock, among other scenes. While the place is as shabby as the bison hide draped on the wall that they can run their glitter-flecked hands through, I hope the students will be able to embody a little of their school's namesake and his powers of perception in finding those authenticating details he worked so well into his poems. Somehow, Ted's managed to sneak in behind the lethargic students and teachers without them noticing. His hand hovers over the buttons that will bring this tomb to life again for a brief time. Tap, then he's gone.

My Poetry Foundation

The August afternoon I sat in downtown Watertown scribbling out poems on a park bench, I listed what I saw: coffee shop, bookstore, art supplies, stone and brick buildings, brewery, shiny white building. The latter's white ceramic tiles suggested tension; the Medical Arts Building seemed so different than its bulky neighbors. The tiles didn't fit well, and it featured some fancy but cracked fixtures, like jewelry on the building's façade. I was in Watertown to participate in a *plein air* gathering organized by Northern Prairie Arts. As South Dakota's new poet laureate, I was tasked with "writing the prairie" just as the participating painters were "painting the prairie." The downtown area held more charm for me, though.

Perhaps it was the painting and poetry combination, perhaps the nostalgia summoned by back-to-school weather, perhaps it had been *The Poetry Home Repair Manual*, which I'd just reviewed to prepare for the approaching semester; in any case, Ted Kooser's example of how to observe details hovered in my mind as I studied the building. His poetry taught me to curate images from my environment and cultivate possibilities for wonder and imagination from experience. As my professor, he'd reminded me that writers need not live in an exotic location or a bustling metropolis to discover writing material; day-to-day life provided fertile ground from which to grow delicious poetry if one knew how to look.

As I wrote about the Medical Arts Building, I recalled Ted's description of a poem as an invitation to a reader to see in a fresh way, and I remembered the story about why he valued this aspect of poetry. A woman had reported to Ted that she couldn't look at a snowy ditch without seeing it through the lens of one of his poems, and that change delighted her. That, Ted said, was a good enough reason to send poems out—to offer new ways of looking at the world, to "lift life." He'd certainly done that for me. Each poem in *Delights & Shadows* conveyed insight, and even now when I see someone trudging across campus wearing a heavy backpack, I think of "Student." An interesting button takes me to "A Jar of Buttons." What fresh perspective could I offer about the Medical Arts Building? I returned to how it contrasted with its neighbors, and the word *bridal* surfaced. When I realized the building seemed too old to be a new bride, I had the first line.

The whole poem came together that afternoon on the bench, even though I usually revise across weeks and months. There were longer versions where I listed more details, where I imagined the building's historical context, and where I brought my experience of selecting a dress for my second wedding, but I settled on a distilled version of those. During a tutorial my first semester at UNL, I'd brought Ted a poem based on a childhood memory—my mother and I watching TV curled up in a gold, velveteen-upholstered recliner. Ted challenged my adjectives: "Why does it matter if it was gold? Could it have been brown? Pink?" I defended the draft too much, but in the verbal wrestling match over adjectives that Ted won handily, I learned the importance of brevity—every word for a reason.

Ted's response to my drafts, his own literary examples, and his keen, compassionate, and witty disposition as a professor transformed my understanding about poetry-writing life and established a new foundation. Writing had meant a constant scrambling for inspiration but shifted into an ever-evolving practice of stretching my perceptions. Craft became a diligent form of play. Sound became an inquiry into meaning. And teaching these principles to my students became a way to bring the joy of writing practice to others as Ted had brought it to me.

Medical Arts Building, Watertown

Like a second-time bride,
she wears white well even
if self-conscious—porcelain
tiles dimpled. Still, adorned
with understated ornament
in the midst of rough and bulk,
she shines.

Prunings

for Ted

If you want to find his poems,
Go out to the old tool shed

And back by the west wall
Look for some prunings he left

For the mice and barn swallows.
They're there under the weeds,

Where the honeysuckle
Blazes in the evening light.

. . .

Upon his return to Ithaca, Odysseus looked out over his home-
land and asked three fundamental questions: "What land is this?
What community? What people live here?" For more than fifty
years, Ted has been answering these questions, his rich, mem-
orable poems, so eloquent and rewarding in their revelations,
creating a long and lasting legacy of one our nation's true literary
treasures.

Inland Sea

Pierre, SD, 1961

Your little brother gets squirmy in the grocery cart,
so your mother lifts him out, gives you money for two
boxes of animal crackers, saying you can take him
next door to the five and dime; she'll come find you
when she's done. You pay and wait for change to put
in your pocket, then take his hand and pull him past
the gumball machine at the front window, reminding
him what's over at Ben Franklin's. No trees on Main,
sun prickling your foreheads, blank sky meeting ground
between the few buildings and containing them, their scant
shade in this place where horizon surrounds on every side.
You pull the glass door open with both arms, and a bell
rings above the two of you; the clerk looks up to watch
you wander down the creaky wooden toy-aisle—eyeing
slinkys lined up on a shelf and paddleboards with balls
on rubber bands, bins of marbles, jacks, pretend watches,
silly putty, small wind-up monkeys and clowns and plastic
spheres full of jumping beans—slowly passing them all
without stopping, making your way toward the quiet
at the back of the store where the big bubbling aquarium
glows unearthly blue. You drop your brother's hand
and he steps close to it, nose at the glass, pointing and
tilting his head up, gradually lowering his voice to
near-whisper, not remembering the box he holds by its
string handle and would normally open right away,
identify sweet animals to devour. Together you watch
all the different little rippling shapes and colors of fish

whose names you can't read but have asked about many times, and you've helped him memorize—angelfish, rabbitfish, rainbows, betas, mollies, platies, neon tetras weaving in and out of each other hypnotically, shifting in groups around pretend sunken ships and sandcastles, tall waving weeds and half-open treasure chests. You make up for him hushed stories of where in the world the graceful creatures might've come from, who must have found them, at what depths, how old the tiny beings might be, how wise, no matter what strange place they find themselves in now, place you stand in forgetting, so far from any kind of sea. Once at the farm, down by the creek, you found rocks with shells in them and took them back to show your uncle. He said some think long ago the prairie was a giant ocean with fish many times the size of people, and there were no people anywhere.

. . .

Ted Kooser's work has been a touchstone for me. "Inland Sea" was written in gratitude for Ted's honoring of the Great Plains, his keen attention to what often goes unnoticed, and his skill in navigating the borders between place and consciousness, between clarity and mystery.

The Work at Hand

You wake from the dream uncertain
if you are living in this world or the next,
pretty sure that no one is dreaming you
but unsure if someone might be dreaming

this world, watering the flowers, shaping
the clouds, and watching the birds
build their nests, a skill or art or craft—
a beautiful necessity—while we inhale

and exhale the deep breath of our days
our anonymous days our days
of shopping lists and headlines
the days that we dream ourselves

up and out the door and
on our way to work and what is
our work but to scatter the seeds
and dream ourselves whole?

. . .

I met Ted when I was the director of the Haystack Mountain
School of Crafts in Deer Isle, Maine, and invited him to be a
visiting writer for a two-week session in the summer of 2005. He
and I had the opportunity to visit the saltwater farm where E.
B. White had lived in nearby Brooklin. I remember the two of
us standing in the small boathouse where White had written his
elegant essays. We were like two pilgrims. I have long admired

Ted's ability to see what is profound in the everyday and the way he can find grace in the details. "The Work at Hand" is about our daily lives and what perhaps our task is—to make things whole.

Absorbing the Moment

Ted Kooser was my professor, a member of my PhD dissertation committee, and—when I was selected in the fall of 2009 to be the editorial assistant for American Life in Poetry—my mentor and "boss." Ted is still my mentor: whenever I'm working on a short poem or flash nonfiction and need to exercise brevity, I often ask, "What would Ted do?" And who doesn't ask the same question when wandering at home, puzzling over a life question? I only partly joke. Posing, "What would Ted do?" to the ether is not uncommon whenever I'm stuck in a quandary and need a succinct answer that might already be before me, but I just need to pause, observe with more openness, more awareness, and connect all the dots of the moment to reveal it.

Although I first started working with Ted as a UNL graduate student in the fall of 2008, the first time I met Ted was a couple years before, during a summer writers' workshop in Duluth, Minnesota. Ted was teaching poetry, but I was adventuring in fiction and excited to be a student in Robert Olen Butler's workshop. Still, it was no secret among some of the workshop organizers that I wanted to learn more about writing poems, about precision, and about studying with the recent U.S. Poet Laureate.

My shyness gets the best of me in most situations. I'm shy around people I haven't met who aren't poet laureates, so needless to say, days leading into that summer's writers conference, I hadn't said a word to Ted. When the conference social event arrived and everyone from all genres settled at the director's lovely Victorian home with sprawling porch and backyard full of flowers and a stream, my workshop roommate (who was studying poetry with Ted) nudged me and said this was the perfect casual moment to ask Ted about poems. Or maybe she said, "about life."

The social was dreamlike and dragonfly-then-firefly filled. My roommate said Ted was out on the front porch, and so, shyness softened, I went out front. The porch was massive, though it might have grown with memory. There was a porch swing, and there was Ted sitting quietly upon it. And I joined him. The swing was massive, grand, and painted some pastel color. Maybe blue. I probably asked some awkward question regarding poems. What does a shy person taking a fiction workshop and feeling poetry-inadequate ask Ted Kooser? Actually, I probably wasn't as prepared as that, however bumbling. I probably said, "Hello, hey nice swing!" That seems right. Whatever the words of introduction, I remember a comfortable silence, swinging on a wide swing on a massive Victorian (cape? colonial?) porch, both our leg sets kicking in the air beneath swing seat and porch floor. I'm sure I was beaming. I tried my best to absorb the moment. Inwardly I repeated: *I'm swinging on a porch swing with Ted Kooser.* We continued swinging in silence. I continued to beam. Ted commented on the fireflies. They were cinema-quality that summer night. I think we talked about Nebraska and maybe Upper Michigan, certainly Lake Superior, possibly the prairies—where we came from to gather where we were. And we talked a bit about writing. I don't remember either one of us being genre-specific. What stays with me—not just from that summer porch swing moment, but from the poetry tutorials, dissertation meetings, and American Life in Poetry discussions I had with Ted at UNL—was the idea of absorbing the moment. The value of it. Being in it. Imprinting it as best as we humans can do. Connecting the dots that exist within and that extend outside and beyond the memory, the snapshot we take of all the sights and sounds and tactile imagery. When I read Ted's poems, I imagine the moment of observation that might have served as inspiration or catalyst for the written lines. When I try to write my own "Ted Kooser-ish" poem, I do the same: I mine my memories and snapshot observations. I try connecting the dots. I try extending them: lines of reach become lines of poem, and past observation becomes present moment of awareness.

Ode to the Poster of Reptiles & Amphibians
on the Exam Room Wall at the Animal Clinic
on South Street

It shows no judgment, with its smears
of Nolvasan solution and earwax globs—aqua
blue splotched by brown—covering the spines
of lava lizards. Doesn't say, *how do you stay*
furless in Nebraskan winters where the wind
would blow your scales? No. None of that.
When the Pekingese in the room next door yelps
out its thermometer probe, I swear the tattered tip
of poster flicks up a salamander's several eyelids.
Distraction for sure, while the tech inserts the needle
above a tortie paw, while the mews, so faint, slow
to acceptance. While I stroke her fur and we both
forget the winter outside, this place we've come to,
this place today, together, we'll forever depart.

GERALD COSTANZO

Conversing with Ted Kooser for Nearly Fifty Years

Ames High aims high
—T.K.'s high school slogan

Mustang born, Mustang bred,
Gonna be a Mustang till I'm dead.
—G.C.'s high school slogan

The first thing he ever told me (1972)
was of his intention to spend his adult life
as a non-attorney spokesperson
and that fastened our friendship.
Most of what we've said to each other
is none of the general public's

business, but I am at liberty
to divulge that what has been taken
to be an apocryphal tale

Ted has always
professed about my fixation
with the hideous color

Van Dyke Brown is accurate
absolutely.
Usually we have agreed to agree—

our mutual fascination with "Storage
Wars" for instance (Justin paws his way
through a decent locker, etc.).

On a dull day in the summer
of 1986 Ted admonished
Never water willows on Wednesdays,

(I wrote this down) and in November,
1997 he cautioned, *If you're gonna resort
to playing solitaire, Jerry, you can*

only beat yourself.
Always amiable and cheeky, on July 4,
2012 he opined, *Were walking*

*wildly beneficial to one's health,
mailmen would be immortal,* and
last week as we faced each

other on Zoom,
Just who, he wanted to know—*in
the gigantic fullness of time—has been*

*more roundly disregarded,
forsaken and forgotten than the
Unknown Soldier's wife?*

. . .

"Conversing with Ted Kooser . . ." is a quasi-satirical reenactment
of hundreds of conversations—in person, on the telephone, and
via email—between Ted and me over nearly half a century. We have
discussed everything and everyone. Among countless others, I have
admired him for his intelligence, great poems, sense of humor,
abiding humanity, as well as for his lengthy service to poetry and to
literature both for children and adults. I have known very few peo-
ple who fit the description I would attribute to Ted: he's *authentic.*
At the risk of seeming to be sentimental, I'd say his friendship has
been one of those rare gifts that make life worth living.

BARBARA CROOKER

Forsythia

What must it feel like,
after months of existing
as bare brown sticks,
all reasonable hope
of blossoming lost,
to suddenly, one warm
April morning, burst
into wild yellow song,
hundreds of tiny prayer
flags rippling in the still-
cold wind, the only flash
of color in the dull yard,
these small scraps of light,
something we might
hold on to.

. . .

This is a poem that Ted inspired (although really, he's been an inspiration for all of my work). What I love about Ted's work is that it's as clean and clear as a glass of fresh water, work that sustains, poems I return to again and again.

TODD ROBINSON

Broken Summer Sonnet

after Naomi Shihab Nye

Each day I miss the Keya Paha braided
   with sandbars, birds and bugs stitching
songs to summer mornings. I miss the soft
   bend of road under cottonwoods, that rotten
zipline to the far unknowable shore, cousins
   slogging endless beanrows, pulling a pipe
for riverwater, tractor plopping along ahead of us.

Forever I miss my uncle the dirt farmer working
   a toothpick between gone teeth—his bronchitic
chortle in tv light. Forever I miss my aunt's hands
   ruffling my soft hair, sending me to read
comic books under cottonwoods in the farmhouse
   yard before time took it all away. I miss the Keya
Paha sun-warmed knee-deep whispering stay.

. . .

Ted always said not to put a poem's form in the title: "If you title your poem 'Sonnet for Susan,' somebody's going to get persnickety and start counting syllables and stresses, expecting an actual sonnet, and if you falter in the form, they'll write off your poem." Forgive me, Ted, but I like the alliteration of "Summer Sonnet," and I thought the "Broken" did double duty in mourning what's gone (a specialty of yours, if I'm reading you right) and in announcing the plentiful flaws to follow. Forbear my cheek, if you can! P.S. The "braided" in line one is lifted right from your and Jim Harrison's *Braided Creek*, the greatest poetical correspondence since Li Po and Tu Fu.

Menagerie

She bought my sister a rat that spent evenings
on our living room couch bent over a bowl

of macaroni and cheese, gave my brother
a parakeet that admired itself in mirrors

until it flew into a window. My mother came home
from the county fair with a goldfish

that swam through a castle and an iguana
who lived under a heat lamp with a wilted

sliver of lettuce. If there were free kittens
in a box downtown I was allowed to bring them

home in my coat pockets. She loved creatures:
serpentine, bovine, terrestrial, herbaceous.

She had grown up on her grandfather's farm,
kept the tiniest swine in her childhood bedroom

where she fed them from bottles,
admired their grunts and stiff hair.

She bought my daughter a tarantula
with velvet legs and my nephew three toothy

Shih-Tzus, bred, she said, to warm the feet
of emperors. At the end of her life she came home

with a goat that devoured the back yard
and slept on our overturned canoe, his beard

lifted by a gentle wind.

. . .

I have always felt an affinity for Ted Kooser's poems, which notice the man "singing to himself in the doctor's crowded waiting room" or the reader with "her hair still damp at the neck" wearing "a raincoat, an old one, dirty from not having enough money for the cleaners." In his shimmering poetry, "a galaxy dies" while a farmer "snaps on his yard light." Kooser has published a couple of poems about my family in his column American Life in Poetry, which, like "Menagerie," pay attention to the gorgeous, surprising ordinary world: a world he and I both inhabit on the page.

On Ted Kooser: Poet of Clarity & Sight

Pulitzer Prize–winning poet Ted Kooser's writing is the purest form of poetry. He begins with a crystalline image that builds to a shimmering perfection resonant with meaning and gravitas. Like William Carlos Williams, Gwendolyn Brooks, Walt Whitman, and Henry David Thoreau, Kooser invites us to slow down, look closer—to make use of stillness and resonant imagery to experience communion with the deepest part of ourselves and the world we inhabit. Consider his poem, "Abandoned Farmhouse," which from the close image in the first lines creates a sharp acuity intertwined with religious themes:

> He was a big man, says the size of his shoes
> on a pile of broken dishes by the house;
> a tall man too, says the length of the bed
> in an upstairs room; and a good, God-fearing man,
> says the Bible with a broken back
> on the floor below the window, dusty with sun;
> but not a man for farming, say the fields
> cluttered with boulders and the leaky barn.

From this opening, Kooser moves outward to an exploration of absence and loss, uneasy and haunting. The repetition creates a rippled echo that resonates with both intensity and softness.

Ted Kooser is a naturalist not just of nature, but of every aspect of our world. Looking and watching are his legacies—his words echoing with the still bone-deep clarity of a crisp winter's day just after the first deep snow, unswept and sparkling in the sunrise.

"Afterwards" is my attempt to humbly take these aspects of Ted Kooser's work I enjoy so much and create my own poem. I begin with an image that has long haunted me since girlhood— that of the three men thrown into the furnace's flames by yet another mad Old Testament king because of their still certainty of belief.

Afterwards

it is only the lack
of heat, the lack of singed

skin   and hair ashed
to fill the nostrils in

the coolness of the dewed
morning air below the unfurled

sounding of their winged
rhythm rippling the air unfired
that is remembered. this,

the stuff of miracles
that dreams are made of.

they never talk of how
now   you run from flame

how   you cannot cook dinner
how   you cannot see any color but

red. eyes stinging memory
closed, the inferno still blazes

& you hear the cackling sizzle
& you think you see your skin

blackening, pulled from
your bones like a

chicken on a spit crisped
    from the firing   in

these night sweats
    & shivered terrors.

these fever dreams
    constant &

enflamed in this still
    loudening   echo.

The Mechanic

Ted liked "Turning 32," as I recall. He liked "their mistakes / which look to me like filmy windows." I remember he tinkered with the "what we possess / turns into a debt we owe," a line that was more equivocal until Ted told me to go for it. He helped me fix the last stanza, too, though his suggestions for change always fit so seamlessly with my idea of what the poem could be that I can't remember what we changed now. Like a repair so deft you can't tell where the original fault line was.

Most of all, I remember how he respected and shared the grief of my miscarriage with me, how he shared my excitement when I became pregnant again. "You're getting secret knowledge of the world, now," he said.

Ted's office was a place of magic for me for the few years that I did tutorials with him. It was a long room, with a desk crowded in the corner and an old desktop computer sat atop it. At the other end, there was a comfortable couch. There was a large window that looked out into the swirling Nebraska snow. He lit the space with lamps so the glow was warm and close.

It was a place outside of the most confusing and stressful parts of school for me; a place where the work of poems was at the forefront, outside of their value or mysterious use to me in getting me a job. I thought of Ted as a poem's mechanic, and the poem as a little machine producing wonder, mystery, emotion. I could take a poem to the mechanic and watch him peer into it, peer down into its works and pick out the part that made it most itself, refining it. I could take a poem to him and watch him subtly shift a part so that it stopped making a funny noise. He was a brilliant tinkerer. He seemed to see straight down into the body of the poem in a way I deeply respected and admired—he admired a good image, he admired the music of the line, and he admired sentiment simply put. He deeply respected the mystery that arose in the course of writing, the surprising element of the poem that a poet might not see herself, until an astute reader pointed it out.

Our meetings together also took on elements of the mysterious. One day, we might talk about his favorite kind of pencil (a Koh-i-Noor variety, no longer made, with quite soft graphite that glides in shadows across the page), and he would sketch me a little drawing with the pencil ("the edge of town, for Katie") on a postcard made of heavy cardstock. I've framed and kept it next to my bed, ever since. He gave me the pencil, too, even though he told me he had to scour eBay for old boxes of them.

One day, a perfect fall day with all the trees on fire with red and orange, I found him wracked with love. "Every fall, I lie in the grass and ask for one more October," he said.

One day, I ran in, underslept and underfed, as I always was, and he asked if I was hungry. I nearly nipped his finger in reply.

"I'll see to your poem, and you see to these cookies," he said, handing me a tin of homemade cookies one of his admirers had made for him. "Eat all you want."

One day, I walked in, and there was a large animal reclining on his couch at the back of the office.

"I got that coat in the '70s, and thought I'd give it to one of my students. He doesn't have a winter coat," Ted said.

"That's not a coat," I said. "That's a bear." I went over to pet it, feeling wildly jealous of the student who was getting such a weird gift from such a wonderful person.

"Do you want to try it on?" Ted said, seeing me admire it.

"Sure," I said. It hung down to my ankles and was covered in ugly faux fur. I did a little dance around the room, before removing it to its resting place on the couch, where it presumably fell asleep again.

"You always carry the air of someone ready to be astonished by something," Ted said to me once. But I think I was only that person around Ted, and now that I don't take tutorials with him, I am disappointed to report that I find the world 50 percent less astonishing. The best poets carry you into wonder with them; they aid and abet the glory of the world. That is Ted.

Turning 32

At this age, my mother had an eight-year-old
and a one bedroom, and my father was gone:
halfway to go on his sentence for robbery,

and what I have this morning looks like nothing
they had, though my life is made from the bones
of those lives, and my body too: his bad teeth,

her full mouth, her tendency to rage, his endless,
restless need—Bless them. Bless their mistakes
that lately look to me like filmy windows.

I have no property, no money; I have a dog who
paces the night in time to my dreams; a man
who rubs my back every morning to remind him

of the shape of me, forgotten in his nightly swim
in the unconscious. I've lost a baby. I am making
another, I am sick with it; the fear and wonder daily

strike me dumb. It goes on, I am sick with it.
My parents: I look back and back and see their fear
which is my own; their hearts, which are mine;

we beat the same: tympanic, achy. What we possess
turns into a debt we owe. Before he left, my father
drove me through winters on the back of his bicycle.

He wrapped me in thick clothes to keep me warm.
He asked me could I hold the Blockbuster bag for him,
and I was four and I said *No. Okay,* he said, and wrapped

my scarf tighter. Now, my mother calls to tell me
she cannot fathom a grandchild. She says *I know it's wrong,*
but it's as if you, who are mine, are making something else.

It's mine! she laughs. Last week, I saw the heartbeat.
It flutters like a verdant plant in the chest.
That's mine, I thought, and prayed for her forgiveness.

Summer Morning Walks:
4 Postcards for Ted Kooser

1.

The *wish you were here* of the world
calls again as I wander the streets
an hour past dawn: mourning
dove *coo*, squirrel chatter, white tail
of rabbit disappearing beneath
the shade of ferns. Clouds move east,
dispersing their menace, and on the lawn
of a stranger, a sign of the times,
staked before a stand of hydrangeas:
Be at Peace, Beloveds—
though few of us, these days, are.

2.

"It might not be such a bad thing," you once said,
"if everyone was trying to write poems."
One could do far worse with one's time,
I know—and we all know many have. Perhaps
poetry might entice these boys on the corner inside
to count pentameters on their fingers instead
of trying to blow them off with the cherry bombs
they're already *booming* the neighborhood with
at 8:00 a.m. because this is the birthday of freedom, and
that, apparently, calls for some noise. America continues
to sing like Whitman—contradicting itself at every turn.
Endlessly optimistic. Just as endlessly in denial.
And later, there will be a barbecue and the red glare

of bottle rockets aimed toward the moon—which is waxing
toward full and will do its silent best to outshine.

3.

Sometimes the delights are *in* the shadows,
or it's the shadows that delight—like this
stretch of city sidewalk dappled into lace
below the locust trees lining the curb.
Above a storm drain, a fish straight out
of the Pleistocene is etched into the concrete
reminding us where all water runs eventually.
Ocean feels like little more than abstraction
when you're so far from any shore, meandering
in the Big Middle, though the sky stretches
limitless with a few stray clouds rippling
like waves I can ride into another day.

4.

If there are any laurel trees in Garland, Ted,
you might make yourself—well—a garland,
or just snip yourself a sprig and tuck it,
like one of those jaunty little feathers, into the band
of your favorite hat. Take your place at the best table
in that little café in Dwight to while away
the morning, sipping weak coffee and writing
postcards addressed *to whom it may concern*—
meaning, of course, everyone.
Remind us: *You would love it here*—
meaning, of course, the world.

STACEY WAITE

The Politics of Noticing: Ted Kooser
in Poetry and Pedagogy

Ted Kooser was drinking chocolate milk from a bottle. The young aspiring poets at Young Writers Camp—a youth program I started at the University of Nebraska in 2012—kept repeating this in a kind of disbelief. *Did you see he was drinking chocolate milk?* And they'd emphasize the word *chocolate* as if that detail were a shimmering sign of Ted Kooser's humanity and his connection to the fifteen- and sixteen-year-old writers who could not believe a poet laureate of the United States was sitting before them in a college classroom desk, drinking *chocolate* milk and taking them through a writing exercise that was itself meant to illuminate the power of a small detail and how to compress that detail, strip it down to its essential parts.

On first glance at both Kooser's work and the writing exercise he did with the youth poets that day, one might think we are talking only about issues of craft, that we are deep in the territory of poet skills: building an image, sharpening one's language. And these are certainly gifts of craft we can receive from Kooser's work, from his stunning and distilled image-making to his precise and concise diction. There is no shortage of work that celebrates these aspects of Kooser's poetry. But I am more interested here in talking about the ethics and politics of Kooser's ability to *notice*, something he told the youth poets was essential to *being* a poet. The ability to notice, to see what is in front of you in its simplest and clearest way.

When I first arrived on the Nebraska campus, just one month after I had earned the degree that even made me eligible to take a job as a professor at a university, I walked past Ted Kooser in the English building where we both worked. He smiled at me, stopped to chat. And afterwards, I immediately ducked into a doorway to text my closest poet friend, telling him, "I seriously just talked to Ted Kooser in a hallway." It was the kind of moment that made me truly understand the youth poets' obsession with his *chocolate* milk. He was just walking and talking to me—in that quiet Ted Kooser way.

I was so nervous to even ask him to visit my creative writing camp for kids in the summer, despite his reputation of being so generous with his time and so kind to his colleagues. But when I finally got the nerve to ask him, he was thrilled at the invitation. And he showed up with a pile of poetry books to read from . . . and that glistening bottle of chocolate milk. One of the students asked him to read "Flying at Night." And Kooser obliged:

> Above us, stars. Beneath us, constellations.
> Five billion miles away, a galaxy dies
> like a snowflake falling on water. Below us,
> some farmer, feeling the chill of that distant death,
> snaps on his yard light, drawing his sheds and barn
> back into the little system of his care.
> All night, the cities, like shimmering novas,
> tug with bright streets at lonely lights like his.

I remember feeling the awe of the moment. Me, a new professor who had only lived in cities—New York then Pittsburgh—listening to my new Nebraska student-writers listen to Ted Kooser read a poem that notices the shared common language of all places, of every place. And yes, as a poet, I could talk forever about the image of a galaxy dying "like a snowflake falling on water." But the melting snowflake makes me think, quite honestly, of something far more important than the tightness of a line, the exquisiteness of a perfect simile. More than that, the poem reminds me (all Kooser's poems remind me) how essential it is to notice, to see the image, to see the connection right in front of you. To see it clearly.

Imagine a world in which we all invested in seeing clearly, a world in which precision matters. We don't live in that world, and Kooser has been asking us to since the 1970s. From my observations of his work with youth poets, and his work with graduate students at UNL, I can say that Ted Kooser is not only a poet who notices but also a teacher who notices: a person who sees other people. Nothing is invisible to Ted Kooser. And over the years of reading his work and knowing him for the past decade, I have come to understand that philosophy—the idea that it is a human being's (and especially a poet's) calling to see clearly—as profoundly political, even though some might argue Kooser's work is grounded in some more neutral territory. His poems (and Ted) do have arguments: about human connection, about the environment, about identity. And perhaps the most profound of these arguments is a call to notice: a call to see and see again (a kind of revision) our world, our language, and our selves.

I've been corresponding with Ted Kooser by email for about
five years, ever since finishing my PhD in Creative Writing at
the University of Nebraska and relocating to the East Coast.
Each time I receive one of his messages, which often end with
the phrase, "More in time," it astounds me that he still so gener-
ously makes time for a former graduate student of his, especially
since I know I'm not the only one. When I was accepted into the
doctoral program at UNL, I wasn't sure at first that I wanted to
attend. I'd heard only glowing reviews from past students and
former teachers, but I didn't think that a poet necessarily *needed*
a PhD to ply her or his craft or to teach. I'd seen Ted Kooser
listed on the faculty but knew that renowned writers might only
teach the occasional semester in a graduate program; there was
a good chance I might never get to work with Ted, much less
see him around campus. Yet when Guy Reynolds, the director
of graduate studies at the time, promised me Kooser was not
only still teaching but also meeting with students one-on-one
each year in what he called a "poetry tutorial," I snapped up
the offer. I knew I couldn't turn down the opportunity to work
with a contemporary master on par with Nobel laureates like
Seamus Heaney, Tomas Tranströmer, and Wisława Szymborska,
but I had no idea just how much the quiet hours spent with Ted
in his office would alter the trajectory of my life.

Looking back, I see now that something had always been calling
me to Nebraska. A few years after finishing my Master of Fine Arts
at the University of Wisconsin–Madison, I received the news with
an equal mix of glee and disbelief that my poetry manuscript, *The
Book of What Stays*, had won the *Prairie Schooner* Book Prize and
would be published by the University of Nebraska Press. Then
a friend recommended applying for a writing residency at the
Kimmel Harding Nelson Center for the Arts in Nebraska City.

Living in Portland, Oregon, at the time and working unhappily in the office of a nonprofit, I said an impulsive *yes* when offered a month at the residency.

During that chilly January in Nebraska City, I walked every day to the local library, which held an entire shelf of signed books by Kooser. Each morning as I tried to write, I pored over his poems centered on daily life in the same Great Plains landscape at which I now stared out as well. By chance, another writer at the residency said she was going to Lincoln—just about an hour away—to do research at the State Historical Society and invited me along. Since my book had won the *Prairie Schooner* Prize, I figured I would thank the people who had chosen the book and take the chance to meet them. After an open-armed welcome from poet Grace Bauer and several PhD students in the program, and after feeling the sense of possibility in Lincoln, I knew I had no other choice. Back at the residency, I locked myself in my studio and completed all the necessary steps to apply, my stack of checked-out Kooser books close at hand. Though I felt my application was a longshot, in less than a year, I would be offered an Othmer Fellowship to study and teach at UNL and would start my work with Ted during the following fall semester.

To say I was nervous before our first poetry tutorial would be an understatement. I remember sweaty palms and a queasy yet excited feeling at the pit of my stomach. Ted's kindness and welcoming presence are legendary in the literary community, even far beyond Nebraska, but I couldn't shake the notion that I would be handing my unfinished poems over to a Pulitzer Prize–winner and former U.S. Poet Laureate, sitting for several silent moments in his office while he read them to himself. Wouldn't that feel like torture? What if my poems never measured up to his high standards? Of course, I had no reason to feel anxious. Ted's honest, gentle manner made sure of that, and I heard later that other graduate students found their time with him so calming, they sometimes lovingly dubbed his tutorials "Therapy with Ted."

But my sessions with him over the years were not always easy or relaxing. My friends from UNL can tell you just how seriously I took those meetings, refusing to go out on the nights leading up to them and sitting alone instead at my kitchen table, revising my poems again and again before I had to hand them over to Ted.

Difficult memories often emerged out of what I wrote during the tutorials: grief from my father's early death from hepatitis C; the challenges of caring for a mother with agoraphobia and multiple sclerosis; the breakup of past relationships. My work with Ted helped to surface the pain I'd pushed down and hidden, trying not to feel it. Given how closely he paid attention to his students' work *and* to their lives, however, there was no avoiding something, even if it lingered just beneath the words on a page. I'd heard other students pushing against this brand of vulnerability, yet I welcomed the invitation into greater authenticity. Our time together taught me how the materials of everyday life, no matter where you live or who you are, can infuse the poetry with a sense of wonder and truth. Ted has often said during poetry readings and meetings with students that he never lies in his poems. I remember one meeting with him when I'd brought in a poem about a visit to Barcelona with my ex. I had made up a trip to Lago Banyoles and fictionalized our time in Spain in an attempt to give the poem more "weight." Gently but firmly, Ted squinted his eyes and looked at me: "Did this *really* happen?" he asked. I was beyond embarrassed at first, yet sensed this was a powerful lesson in telling *myself* the truth too. After that, I knew there would be no fooling him, and I would always be conscious of when I was fooling *myself* in the poems. While other writers might settle for a so-called emotional truth in their work, Kooser has always argued for an accurate representation of the world exactly as it appears to us. Maybe that's why each of his own poems feels as solid and trustworthy as a pocket watch, useful for daily living and made of real materials.

Perhaps more than anything else, though, Ted's selfless generosity stands out for those of us fortunate enough to have spent time with him at the University of Nebraska. Ted wrote to me recently to say that he'd just cleaned out his office and turned in his keys, retiring for the second time in his life. I couldn't help but sense a bittersweet tone in his note. Ted Kooser has given of himself completely to the students who passed through his office in Andrews Hall year after year for decades, and I am honored to have sat in that same armchair where so many others waited as he silently read the work, absorbing every word. It's staggering to consider how many lives Ted's poems and teaching have affected, and I think of what Maya Angelou once said about the mark we might leave behind: "Your legacy is what you do every day. Your legacy is every life you've touched." With his down-to-earth wisdom and humor, Ted taught us to be ourselves above all else, to be true to our own lived experience—joy and sorrow, love and fear alike—so that we might make the most of our limited time on earth.

More in Time: A Letter to Ted

Each of us already knows how to shelter
in place, exchanging messages
from our respective villages, our words
tracing unseen paths on the air
from Nebraska to Vermont, and back.
I like to think of you stepping out
on the dirt road you walk each day
at the same time I begin to walk mine,
paying close attention because of you
to black-eyed Susans nodding
their yellow heads in a nearby field,
and the rustle of maples above,
sending down a second rain from
the tips of leaves, having saved a small
kiss of water for the very instant
I passed under to receive that blessing.
And I think of how you often end
your emails with the same promise—
More in time—though I can't help
reading it as another of your teachings,
that there will be so much more
delight in my days, hours, and minutes
if I learn to pause, for instance,
by the side of the road and listen
to the scuffling of a painted turtle's
clawed feet plodding across
loose gravel to reach the creek,
until I—seeing you do the same
for each of us with your poems—
lift him to safety on the other side.

Good Morning

I've woken up at 4:30 just for you, Ted. I'm generally not someone who wakes up at 4:30, but here I am, smelling the cinnamon in my oatmeal while my green tea cools in a mug decorated with the skyline of San Antonio. From where I sit at the small kitchen table, when I look out the window, I mostly see myself reflected back. There's the vague outline of trees barely backlit with what I'm guessing is the first sign of eastern sunlight. This hour's not my best. My dog stands near the backdoor, wanting out. I wonder if you're up now, too.

When we first met, just a month or two after I moved away from my home state, I was interested in writing poems that looked outward, but in the years since working with you I've begun to understand I was only trying to avoid talking about myself. I come from a long line of Texas talkers—tall-tellers, weather-ramblers, people who don't mind sharing their stories no matter how long they take. My whole life at home, getting a word in was difficult. So at some point early on, I decided it was easier not to. The first time I handed you a poem to read in your office, I felt just as hesitant to speak about myself. But after you told me your thoughts, we kept talking. About our lives, the weather, why I needed to try a Runza. We weren't rambling. Our speech was measured. Week after week, our talks would cover all kinds of ground, and sometimes you'd show me your notebook, your drafts and drawings filled with bits you'd collected from around your life. Years later, I'm realizing I've become a collector, too, and that I don't mind sharing a bit about myself, either.

Outside the kitchen window, somewhere in the yard, my dog is likely sniffing the fence line or chewing on a pink frisbee. All I hear inside is the faint buzz from appliances because I'm listening for something else. I've heard that a family of coyotes has been roaming our neighborhood. I've been wondering if one was responsible for the dead oriole in the poem I'm making for you. My dog's not a big dog, which is why I'm listening as I write. When I look out, I can see the morning light has grown slightly stronger behind the trees, but mostly I notice how unkempt my hair and beard have grown.

My mother, whom I love dearly, is one of those people who will talk you into a three-minute detour about how many green beans Grandma ate with her chicken-fried steak last week at Alamo Cafe. My mother's always thought quietness to be impolite, that it needs to be filled with talking. It's come to my attention that this backdrop of being surrounded by long, effortless talkers was what brought me to the distillation found in poetry, to the silence in the margins of that measured speech. What I've loved learning from you and your writing is how a poem has to be considerate of its reader, and part of that consideration is not wasting your reader's time. Now, I'm lucky to keep learning from your poems, how they warmly greet their reader, say what they have to say, and end before becoming impolite. But as readers this keeps us coming back—even with your shortest poems, we sure want to keep thinking about them, for much of their art lives in the subtleties. That's why after years of returning to my favorites of yours, they haunt me more than ever.

My dog whines at the door, wanting in. I've heard nothing from the family of coyotes. Instead, there's occasional birdsong. When I glance out the window, morning has really started coming on. Against the pale blue, some pinkish-gray clouds. The trees are more defined, and I can make out the back deck, the neighbor's house. In the window, I'm barely there. Later, I plan to repair another poem I'm working on. It's about me, my daughter, my late father. It's about shoveling snow. I'm trying to see each of these equally, and I'm considering how best to say it, without any spare parts.

The Oriole

after Ted Kooser's "The Mouse"

On the side of our weed-eaten driveway

my young daughter and I find an oriole's head. It's summer,

the world gone scared outside and in,

and the oriole's head a part of all that confusion—

for now, the only part. The head

angled upward as though about to fly its absent body

out from the concrete, and the beak

splayed, lodging a silent squawk

toward us, this last moment preserved

like something from a crude museum

forgotten by an old city—a shriek, my daughter thinks, surely,

shrouding the eyes and softer parts of the head

still missing. This omen resting flat

against the slab, as if in defiance

of it, too, becoming part of that uncarved statue.

Holmes Lake

I've forgotten what it feels like to be wanted
the way the Labrador near me wants the stick

his owner throws for him, his body crashing
into the water before pausing, mouth clapped tightly

around the wet bark, to stand turned, awestruck,
toward the setting sun. On the shore, a father

holds his daughter and twirls a piece of long grass
between his fingers as they watch the hills turn glassy

and bright. I sit beneath a tree and watch them all—
dog and owner, man and daughter—and I feel

far away. And it's here that often I see a fisherman
anchored to one particular spot, ice chest and gear

beside him, his blue windbreaker puffed
from air coming off the water as he eats spoonfuls

of beans from a can, pulls hard on a cigarette,
and adjusts his lines. On those days, I wonder

if he wonders what I'm writing the way I wonder
what he does with the fish he catches—who

he shares them with, if anyone, and whether it's him
who picks the bones clean from the flesh, him

who warms the skillet and lays the fish gently
in the crackling oil. Today, though, the girl's mother

stands in the fisherman's usual spot, her phone
poised, snapping a photo every time the light shifts

a little more to darken the clouds gathering
like flies along the fur of the horizon.

I'm reminded of the horse I used to care for
and how, a month before he died, I found him

standing in the round pen behind the barn
with his head raised, eyes turned toward the sun rising

across the valley while the starlings in the hedgerow
gathered in sound before bursting from the trees

all at once, the air suddenly swarming, the horse
tilting his head to watch their departure much like

the Labrador now watches the sun across the lake.
And I knew a dairy farmer once who, when a cow

was to be put down, would turn her out into the pasture
one last time to watch the sun set. I wonder

if all these animals look at the sky and see something
that I never will. I think I could spend

my whole life trying to find it.

· · ·

When I showed an early version of "Holmes Lake" to Ted, we
spent most of our time talking about the people and the animals

in it. He wanted to know more about the fisherman and the woman taking photos with her phone. And he wanted to know more about me and how I felt as I observed all of this. "I felt far away," I remember saying—a line that eventually made it into the poem. Ted is great at that. He'll single out the thing you're not saying—the thing that, maybe, you've been afraid to say—and he'll ask you, quite simply, to say it.

CONNIE WANEK

Sign Painter

As a young man, Ted Kooser had a job painting signs, which seems to me the perfect employment for an aspiring poet. Each word is costly, and each must be true. Clarity is vital. To communicate is paramount. Also, a sign can say where to go and how far.

More than anyone I know, Ted can be trusted in these matters. And yet, this is only a starting point. It's the "once upon a time" of fabulous stories, none cruel.

How is it that genius is visited upon a certain soul? Do we all have genius in us? I really don't think so. But if we do, then hard work and fidelity to the craft must be even more crucial. Here again, no one surpasses our friend, with his insatiable curiosity and powers of clairvoyance, and with his great store of practical knowledge and his love for his subject, which is life.

Ted has "eyes to see," as the Bible says. He's a very fine artist, too, but I have yet to encounter a self-portrait among his works. Rather, he looks out at the world continually and without pre-conceptions. This might be a Ted Kooser challenge, if you, too, want to write: Try eliminating the word "I" from your work for an entire year. Or a lifetime.

Ted does not filter the world through any religious or polit-ical lens. He doesn't lecture. He offers you the miracle of the imagination, applied to your actual daily life. His poems are open windows to the first spring day, where you can stand in the exhilarating rush of fresh air that enters the winter-stale house.

TWYLA M. HANSEN

I Never Thought I'd Outlive My Evergreens

We planted them along the north lot line,
a seedling windbreak all we could afford,
where cocklebur, sandbur, thistle all thrived
and brome grew taller than those tiny pines.

My father and his father planted trees,
carried water, hope, love through drought years
to slow the wind, shade the farmhouse. Later,
my brothers and I climbed to new heights.

This small woods on city's edge likewise
branched. Kids thrived beneath shades of green,
while disease, drought, time plodded on.
Alone now, I replant with natives.

I'm blue when the living must depart, but my
hope and love, once planted, never die.

. . .

This poem springs sideways from Ted's lines in "January 19—still falling greasy" (*Winter Morning Walks: 100 Postcards to Jim Harrison*), "I thought / for a while last summer that I might die / before my dogs, but it seems I was wrong." From Ted's writings, I learned three poetry essentials: • Brevity and metaphor are next to godliness; • Let no word in your poem go unexamined/ unquestioned/ uninterrogated; • Mortality shadows the sunlight. I was first intrigued with contemporary poetry in the early 1980s when I read the duo poetry collection *Cottonwood County,* by William Kloefkorn and Ted Kooser. Reading through it, the proverbial light bulb snapped on when I realized poems can be written about ordinary, everyday subjects, which led me to classes, workshops, and a writing habit. The rest, as they say, is history.

Sewing Room, 1973

In the hot back room meant to be
a dressing room, as if dressing
should be set apart, there were two
oak chests full of treasures, letters
and jewelry, and a heavy sewing machine,
ancient and, according to my mother,

never quite right. I sat there
on hot summer days, light pounding
from curtainless windows, AM radio
tuned to Gladys Knight and the Pips,
Motown hits, and Diana Ross, who was
the most beautiful woman ever,

and I made school dresses in bright
polyester, the subtle smell of sewing
machine oil an undertow, me in my tank top
and shorts, a sweaty kid taking destiny
in hand, dreaming up a future to the whir
of the open belt and chuffing needle.

. . .

Ted Kooser's deft portrayal of characters, like "Carrie," whose
dusting is never finished, or "Pearl," who has begun to see people
who are not there, has been indelible for me. I have admired his
attention to gesture and detail and his respect for the complexity
of characters' lives. Any influence comes from a reassurance that
the isolated moments and situations of rural life in the flyover
zone are well worth a poet's attention.

Early Wonderment

for Ted Kooser

I love your story from when you were a boy
of how your family was visiting relatives
and you got up from the table after dinner
and wandered out to the back stoop
of the farmhouse and sat there by yourself
listening to the crickets and looking up
at the stars, whose glimmering, I like to imagine,
somehow looked the way the singing
of the crickets sounded, as if their singing
was coming from the stars, or the stars
from their singing—while the muffled voices
from the house behind you drifted out
in familiar intonations. When you looked down
you found that you were not alone:
a big brown toad was sitting next to you,
facing the same direction, toward the fields,
and the two of you sat there for a while
looking together into the night, you said,
"like a couple who had been married so long
that words were no longer necessary."

· · ·

This poem is a reimagining of a paragraph from an interview
Ted did with Judith Harris, which was published in AWP's (the
Association of Writers and Writing Programs) the *Writer's Chronicle*
back in 2010, so in a way I am just a coauthor along with Ted. I
always loved the paragraph, and I cut it out of the magazine and

put it on my refrigerator. Ten years later, while other things have come and gone, it is still on my refrigerator. I've tried to present the story plainly and directly, in a manner that I hope Ted would approve of, but I also added details that he did not mention or that I imagined in the retelling, like the correspondence between the crickets and the stars in the middle of the poem.

Ted Talk

You've got a good angle
on a broken-down barn,

balance your tiny easel
on the steering wheel

and dab a few hours,
the wild plums

of your feelings
turned to color.

Local wonder, you,
who knows why

the town paved
half the road

to the silos.
Valentines you send

by the dozens,
some even in February,

one month
of your winter morning walks

before sunrise,
walks that brought you back

from the no-man's land
of sickness.

All those birds, all those poems
with birds in them,

all those wings and feathers
beaks and claws

and guano. They don't stay.
They lift off into the blue, cranes

that leave us squinting
till we turn back, nod,

and touch one another
with gratitude, with joy.

. . .

When you look up *generous* in the dictionary, it ought to say, "See
Ted Kooser." Even in the most painful moments of grief or sor-
row or rage or suffering, Ted finds words that offer antidotes to
despair. More than ever, we need his enduring poems and essays.

Ted Kooser and the Act of Poetry as Life Practice

While our regions and ethnic/cultural touchstones are practically opposites, Ted Kooser's poetry has always served as an example of how turning an open, loving eye toward the place that made us is not quaint or narrow in scope—it is honest and meaningful, a way for poetry to transcend trends and invite readers to sit down as if for coffee, for intimate conversation.

Ted's tutelage—like his poetry—is straightforward, devoid of pretention, and boldly honest. I was so nervous before our first one-on-one meeting. The forty-foot walk down the institutionally lit hallway felt like miles of dingy beige tile. I was early (which I never am), so I stood in the "lobby" outside his office, going over a freshly written poem and the small notebook of poem titles we were instructed to bring. After a few minutes, a fellow grad student in my cohort stepped out from his office. There was a look in their eyes I couldn't quite place.

His office was large and filled with natural light. The sun pouring from the wide window beside his desk illuminated piles of papers and files and books. One whole wall was a row of tall bookcases filled with poetry, many of which were the work of his famous writer friends (not that he ever pointed that out). It was exactly my film-inspired stereotype of an old poetry professor's office.

It was there in that office that I received advice and guidance that I still remind myself of seven years later: ignore trends and write from the heart; concrete details over explanation always; if you give your poem to the worker at Kabredlo's (a convenience store and gas station I still have never seen in person) and they feel like they "don't get it," it's not a good poem; and lastly, writing is a commitment. He used to say if you write one poem every day for a year, you'll have three hundred shitty poems, thirty-five pretty workable poems, and if you're lucky, the rest will be good, and that's a book. Like his poetry, at the outset, someone might find this to be easy advice because it is straightforward. But also like his poetry, the heart center of following through takes a personal fortitude that I know I certainly have not mastered.

Of all the important things I learned from Ted Kooser during that treasured semester of one-on-one weekly meetings, what meant the most to me was that in our conversations about my poetry, about craft, about publishing, and the different ways a person can navigate their career, we talked about music and family and food and manual labor; we swapped stories about painting buildings and fixing plumbing. He breathed poetry and work and home in the same breath. He modeled that poetry is not separate from or above everyday actions but deeply interwoven into every task, every moment.

Home Again

Chain-linked fence, blinkless red lettering
peddling Anne's Donuts, where we
used to get bear claws in grease-clear bags
and styrofoam cups of watered-down coffee.

In the neighborhood north of the Tower strip,
by the red-doored house, a green oblong
street sign has your name. I text you
a picture and you never respond.

During winter visits, I drive Fresno's wide
North-end streets to remind myself
that boulevards can teem with life: fiery
calendulas, yellow five-fingered pansies,

the grass literally always greener—I do not
miss our concrete side of town, but stay
adjacent, knowing my present doesn't know
how to leave it in the past.

To See Beyond the Self

Ted was the first to nudge "my audience" into my consciousness. I have often mused that I am my first and most important audience because for me poetry became a tool to combat social anxiety, to fulfil the social instinct of humans, to communicate with others, and to maintain a mental balance. In asking me to think of others who may read my work, Ted taught me that the self is an important part of the world but not necessarily its center—that I must exist not in a bubble of language that only I can understand but in one to which the world around me can relate and through which it can access the new realities and perspectives that my own writing brings and adds to it. Ted, in my two tutorials with him, has encouraged me to take a prolonged look at things, to slow down the images of a fast-paced world so that I will instill in myself the ability to appreciate every component and distill the stories that lurk in their darkest edges, which eyes often forget exist.

I remember my first encounter with the poetry of Ted Kooser was in 2014, long before I knew I'd one day learn directly from the man himself, when my friend David Ishaya Osu brought a copy of *Delights & Shadows* during one of our evening walks around the hilly city of Minna, Nigeria, for our weekly poetry rendezvous. He was excited to have found another poet just like Tomas Tranströmer, a poet we both immensely enjoyed and raved about. I was the one who introduced David to Tranströmer the evening he died, before learning of his passing. David enthused that hopefully we would get to meet Ted one day. Well, it goes without saying that I went on to be awestruck each time I pulled up a chair in Ted's office—every session fulfilling David's wish.

When I brought in "Song to a Birdwoman" for my weekly poetry tutorial, Ted pulled a chair close to me and asked that I read it to him out loud as he sat with a pen in his hand, scribbling on his own copy of the poem that he had placed on the face of a book on his lap. It was both hard and exciting for me to read while he jotted down suggestions. Without risking exaggeration, I can say that it was, by far, the most attentive I have ever seen a man.

Ted later asked for my manuscript. I was reluctant to show him the full scope of my grief (the whole thing frightened me as it still does today), but he continued to ask patiently, on two other occasions, until I turned it in—the undented compass of my grief. I wasn't sure where it would lead him, but it only took him a week to get to the end. Ted offered detailed feedback. I was swooning with joy inside my own body and couldn't still my bones from the excitement. Acknowledged and seen, I was humbled.

Ted is a compassionate teacher and mentor who genuinely cares. He will ask about my family, about my health, about how I was adjusting to the bustle of a new country far from home. When I arrived in the U.S., I experienced an immense culture shock that was incredibly difficult to shake off, and it held me back, held my tongue back in my other classes. But each time I was in Ted's presence, I grew fully into myself in ways that weren't so apparent in his absence.

When the pandemic began, Ted and I would exchange emails about how we were coping. I would share poems with him, my thoughts, pictures, and he would do the same, with pictures and his own thoughts. Ted's kindness and generosity didn't exist only as rhetoric—he once expressed his willingness to drive forty-five minutes to the city of Lincoln whenever I would feel the need to talk about poetry or anything else, in between. This was, of course, before the pandemic.

Going back to Tomas Tranströmer, I found a copy of his collected poems on Ted's desk and was shocked to hear he is one of Ted's favorite poets as well. Ted, on learning of my affection for the poet's work, hinted that we should learn Swedish just to do our own translation of Tranströmer's work. I have not put pressure on this to know whether he was serious, or only musing. But between David, Tranströmer, Ted, and myself, the universe set in motion these wheels of poetry long before the first day I met Ted in the flesh.

Song to a Birdwoman

Her mother, labor blood still trickling down her legs
passes her to him, cradled in the towel of her arms,
the hospital waiting-hall full of the baby's face, a hand
glass holding the shrunken reflection of her
mother as of a nursling. The mirror goes back
in time. The moment she sets foot in his palm,
a river of light dispels the night that subdues
the leaves of the neem tree pillared outside.
A wind comes to him and love crosses a strip
of wood, doorsill, windowpane, through
every barricade and bears his body to the night's and
earth's brightest star. The night of her birth,
he sleeps in the car, in the silence of the neem tree
overhead with leaves watered
by a same luring silence. He hungers for her cry,
her first-time voice but she opens her eyes instead,
eyes like she has taken them from her mother's sockets.
Tears furrow his bones, rinse his bones
until he turns pure steed, ready to saddle her on his back.
Eyes dazzle with the excitement of fatherhood,
light falls to that moment as his hair
glints beside the light clenched into a pulpy fist.
This is to the girl rescinding the pitch-dark
so what remains is the value of light, such eternal
seed bearing, same forever through all that makes him
insufficient. He was born into solitariness
that shreds. The moment he began as her father
he roved and only knew his flaxen-flower,
and solemn prayer that he sees her sung up as a birdwoman
gliding into every space that fills the sky.

"Late Summer": Doing the Work and Giving the Gift

I returned to graduate school very late, but from the beginning Ted always made me feel welcome, included, and that I had an important voice in the ongoing conversation about poetry. He made me believe I knew what I was doing, that what I was thinking about was worth sharing. I was also most fortunate to work with him and Patricia Emile as the graduate student assistant to his weekly column American Life in Poetry during 2010–11.

My poem "Late Summer" is emblematic of the two semesters I spent in Ted's poetry tutorial. By the end of the first semester, I was convinced that Ted only had three things at the most to say about a given poem, because he said those three things to me over and over: "This is a little fussy, huh?" "I don't think a lot of people would know what that word is right off the bat." "Now, do you mean for the verb to go there, or there?" I finally realized I was making the same two or three moves, but this poem was a little longer than most that I showed him. I don't quite remember the original impulse of this particular poem, but I do remember Ted taking a long look at the page, pointing at the last few lines, and saying, "This is really good, don't you think? I don't think you need the rest of that up there, do you? I don't even know what that other part is about, do you?" He was right on the money, and I dedicated the poem to him in my collection, *Three Days with the Long Moon*:

LATE SUMMER

for Ted Kooser

From the porch we can see
the tops of children's heads
in the weeds, brown
and yellow mushroom caps.
We wonder what they make
of being there, what old odd jobs
they are doing.

"Late Summer" became a poem of a single moment that also looped
in and encompassed the larger world's awareness within that
same moment, and it is a trait in poetry that I've come to value.

One of the first things Ted told me in our tutorials was that
you'd be pretty lucky if you ever wrote a single poem as recog-
nized and valued as Robert Hayden's "Those Winter Sundays."
I expect that Ted has written any number of such poems. In the
time I have known him, the further his work has progressed,
the more brilliantly it has shone. There is a directness to many
of his later poems that has a near-magic quality. The work is
brave, not pulling a single punch, and yet tolerant. Its language
is nearly flawless, often exhilarating. And as above, it is especially
his gift for encompassing that I most appreciate, as in "People
We Will Never See Again," about a moment in a doctor's office
waiting room:

and he began singing, but softly, the words
to a song that played from hidden speakers
somewhere above our heavy silence,
music we hadn't noticed before he began,
in his whispery voice, to sing for us.

This reminds me of the other question he asked nearly every time we spoke: "What is the gift you are giving the reader in this poem?" He was not insisting that it be a comfortable gift, but at the very least that when we send a poem out into the world, we understand what we are giving—in this poem, an uncomfortable yet comforting reminder of what we're meant to do.

I am grateful for the opportunity to thank Ted Kooser for teaching me to own what I already knew, and that under his tutelage I began to believe: As important as it is to protect yourself, it's far more important to give yourself away, as a writer and as a person. Fashion and status are unimportant. Kindness costs nothing. Give back. If you want to lift your own spirits, do something good for someone else.

And the most important thing: do the best work you can, and do it every day.

At the Rehabilitation Hospital

after Ted Kooser's "At the Cancer Clinic"

A man is being helped by two others
who have placed their arms under each
of his to hoist him from his wheelchair
while a third attaches wide leather straps
to his legs. His upper body is clamped
by his therapist into a black girdle suspended
from a chrome plate above his head.
Two more men attach armbands
and the man clenches perpendicular grips
that must be, it looks to me, welded
onto the metal bars either side of the machine
they're now calibrating to the man's weight.
He's suspended there until his therapist,
who, all this time, has been encouraging him,
calculates ratios and places each of the man's
appendages exactly where she needs them
on the conveyor belt or armrests of this treadmill
they will walk his feet on. One man on each side.
The other three have moved on to set up the boy
with the football injury. — The man, transformed
now to superhero, is on his way to moving his body
of his own accord; the brain being patiently re-taught
by hand. Grace incarnate strolls from machine
to machine checking straps, offering hope, telling
a joke or two. This place is Love, the combined will
of us all, so strong that we've become its legates.

. . .

My son and his wife, Tatiana, rolled their SUV on a highway outside Buffalo, Wyoming, in early spring 2019, and subsequently spent a month in Denver's internationally known rehabilitation hospital, Craig Hospital. At Craig's PEAK Center gym, guided by therapists, volunteers, and family members, patients with traumatic brain and spinal cord injuries relearn ambulation on sophisticated, high-tech machines. The gym provides an added element of therapeutic relief, though, a very real, palpable energy that must be love incarnate. I have never had such a visceral experience of pure, tender compassion. Just walking through the gym's doorway was like entering a *Heavenly* realm, like having an experience of perfect love, what the Greeks called *Agape*. Ted Kooser's poem "At the Cancer Clinic" delivers a similar experience. The speaker conjures for us the love-energy interdependence is capable of creating. I hope my poem conveys a little more of this into the world.

BILJANA D. OBRADOVIĆ

Tribute to Ted Kooser: "A Poem Has to Be Something More Than a Good Story"

I am originally from Yugoslavia (now Serbia), and my first language is Serbian. My father was a diplomat, so that when I was nine we moved to Thessaloniki, Greece, where I began learning English through immersion in an American school, then to Bombay, India, when I was fifteen. After receiving a BA in English from the University of Belgrade, I went to the U.S. in 1988 for graduate study in creative writing. Many teachers and friends, especially in the U.S., have helped me in becoming the poet and writer that I am now. Ted Kooser was especially helpful to me as someone who is not a native English speaker, during a very difficult time for me as well as for my native country. The elegy I wrote in 1999 for my mother seems to me to encompass much of the advice I received from Ted, by being not just a story about my mother's death, but much, much more.

The year after I came to the U.S., my mother got breast cancer, and in 1991, the year I moved to Lincoln, Nebraska, for my PhD, the civil war in Yugoslavia began. My parents came to my MFA graduation at Virginia Commonwealth University in Richmond, but I did not see them for four years, due to the war, after that. Greg Kuzma wrote all over my poems in multicolored pens, Marcia Southwick worked on them more globally, and Hilda Raz edited them, by looking at the details very carefully. I was working on a collection of poems, titled *Frozen Embraces*, which later got published. The unexpected surprise was Ted Kooser's help with my dissertation. I never took a class from him. He was not at UNL much in those days. But he seemed to participate in a lot of the events and often invited graduate students and professors to his house in the countryside where he lived with his wife and had his painting studio. We'd look at his paintings, talk about poetry, drink beer . . . He was very generous with his time.

He offered to look at my poems and spent a week reading and writing eight pages on my dissertation, which I still have, even though my family and I lost many things through Hurricane Katrina. The date on the comments was March 17, 1993. He began with general comments and ended with very specific ones on individual poems. In bullet points, he highlighted the strengths of my dissertation, and here are a few: "The poems all have good clarity and accessibility. The style is conversational and straight-forward. Your spirit is attractive—strong, vital, optimistic, human. The detailing is strong. Any reader should be interested particularly in the details that are unique to your experience, things like pigs and chickens fighting under a tree, the details of life in your country, etc. People feel that they are learning something."

He also gave me things to think about and work on, like grammar issues, tense shifts "so that they call attention to themselves." If I fixed those, then, "the poems would all seem more polished . . . have a better reception." He added that, "Charles Simic's [the Serbian-born, once also U.S. Poet Laureate, with whom I was already in touch at the time] work has a kind of central European consciousness about it, but it is also written in perfectly formed English." He gave one example of using "who" instead of "that" when referring to a person and said that he's "53 years old and [has] been speaking English all [his] life and [he] still miss[es] this one." So he suggested I get "a friend to very carefully go over the poems and tune up the grammar." And I did. I appreciated his honesty.

The biggest issue with the poems, however, he said, was their linear narrative form and that I needed to vary the form of my poems. He noted that some poems in the dissertation were different in form and told me which ones, so that I was "able to do different things in verse." He wanted more of those and added, "My own impulses turn me away from the narrative toward the lyric, which I find more satisfying, and in the lyric I like to see several energies playing forward and back and from either side against each other. My own poems are energies confined not by what is straight ahead of them in time and sequence as in a narrative poem but by their entire nature. To me I succeed best when the interplay of these energies causes the poem to heat up from within and somehow become more than a sum of its separate parts." But he praised me in saying that, "There are . . . ways in which you can use narrative material within a system in which the energies not only go forward but back and sideways as well. You know how to do this and do it effectively in the shorter poems," because I "take a shorter span of narrative and work it harder and examine it more closely," so if I reworked some of the parts in the longer poems (closely scrutinized them), they would be better.

He ended the general comments with, "I think you have a lot of talent and wonderful spirit that comes to make what you write both charming and moving. My feeling is that you need to work harder on each poem to take advantage of every opportunity to tighten and compress and energize." No one has been this straightforward with me before or after.

He went on for six more pages of specific points about individual poems. I took a lot of his advice and appreciated it then and now. He wanted to make sure I started the book with an especially good poem: "First impressions are important." For some he mentioned how I should remove background information, start later in the poem, and end earlier—not to "strain to conclude." Although he mostly praised my endings . . . lots of irony. Most of the time I had good details, and in just a few of them, I had told more, shown less. In another he didn't want me to name the person I was writing about in the poem itself. Ultimately, he said, I had good stories, "but . . . a poem has to be something more than a good story." Such great advice. I wanted this told, as now we are advising our own students, and I hope that we are taking the time to help students in this way, that hopefully they will read carefully, take the advice, and appreciate it, as I have.

Elegy for an Eastern Fallen Star

for Vera, my mother (1932–1999)

Mother's morphine trip, I recall, lasted seven months,
    transporting her to her death. Dad had to lie,
need I mention. He called it "her medication."
    She was ill-prepared (who wouldn't be?) for
that kind of life. None of the treatments worked
    on her, neither did the Orthodox religion
(although faith kept her alive for ten years,
    after she had a vision of St. Petka
who came to her lying in bed, saying she'd protect her,
    then covering her with a blanket and white roses).
I remember when she had been given
    yet another potential cure—
like a member of AA who has lost
    her mind, has drunk Glen Livet Scotch,
thus disturbing her soul, her sacred
    body's temple, or imbibed wine, or Napoleon
Cognac (which she loved to pour into halved
    mangoes when we lived in Bombay).
She felt framed, like an aging Hollywood star,
    now penniless, her skin
stiffening, no more sexual appeal,
    no passing off as a muse of Lord Byron's,
a lighthouse to the stars. She couldn't
    even be in an odd Amish role, beside
red cows, next to a pond with cattails.

Sitting on the toilet, she vomited,
at the same time, then cried and cried, realizing
her chin had begun hardening
on its own, without cosmetic surgery, such tackiness,
while the requiem was being played, and
wreaths of white roses bloomed in the background.

April Wish

Years since we last talked, so today, your birthday,
I'll Teleflora the old lovelies no one thinks to bouquet
or ribbon with satin—bachelor's buttons, chicory,
tiger lilies, even dandelion whose butter brings
a sneeze. I'll tie them in twine for the sake of Nebraska
prairies and sandhills, carpets of bluestem rolling
endlessly to howdy the sky. The memory I keep
by the garden gate in Tennessee, your conversation
with Laddie the sheepdog, intent and private, who
would've gladly heeled you home to the Great Plains,
steering west by northwest. My April wish,
through distance of country: red-candled peonies,
the necessary ants chancing the weather,
an early field of forget-me-nots.

. . .

I began corresponding with Ted in the 1990s and was fortunate to
attend his investiture as poet laureate at the Library of Congress
in 2004. Shortly before heading to Washington DC, he had read
at the University of Tennessee in Knoxville and visited me, where
he bonded with my Shetland sheepdog and gave me wise advice
for my gardens: *Plant for now.* I've taken that advice to heart over
the years, which works both within and outside the garden gate.
In "April Wish," I play off Ted's beautiful poem "Mother."

Ted Kooser, the Midwest Small Press Poetry Renaissance of the 1960s and '70s, and a Poem Inspired by Both

Ted Kooser's Wikipedia site mentions that Ted was part of the Midwestern Poetry Renaissance of the 1960s and 1970s, which he indeed was, especially if one were to add "Small Press" to the title. Large presses had—and for the most part still have—little interest in poetry, long considered a "noncommercial market," so it was small presses such as Ted's Windflower Press and *New Salt Creek Reader* magazine, and, eventually, my own *Dacotah Territory* poetry magazine and later press that, aided by the availability of offset printing, were to play an increasingly important part in what started in the 1960s. A number of us—writers, editors, publishers, and scholars alike—began to find ourselves caught up in something truly exciting, which, if not a renaissance, was certainly a flowering.

The Wikipedia article goes on to quote Warren Woessner as saying the renaissance ended in 1975 with the publication of Lucien Stryk's *Heartland II: Poets of the Midwest.* Stryk's first volume of *Heartland* had been published in 1967 and included work by some of the older or more established poets of the region, such as Thomas McGrath, Robert Bly, James Wright, Mary Oliver, Karl Shapiro, Gwendolyn Brooks, and William Stafford. I certainly don't believe the movement ended in 1975. On the contrary, Stryk's second anthology contained poetry by many of the emerging and younger generation of Midwest writers, such as David Allan Evans, James L. White, Jenné Andrews, and Greg Kuzma (as well as Kooser, Woessner, and myself). Especially for those who remained as working editors well into the eighties, or beyond, Stryk's second volume marked a continuation and new beginning, far from an ending—to say nothing of the increasing number of readings and creative writing classes available in this and other regions.

I grew up in Minneapolis and Kansas City and knew little about rural America, or "the country," as we tended to call it. What brought me to the plains in 1968 was a teaching job in the English Department of Moorhead State College on the western edge of Minnesota, just across the Red River of the North from Fargo, North Dakota, in the broad lakebed of glacial Lake Agassiz—by far the flattest, least populated, and most agricultural landscape I'd ever experienced. To me, as to many, this part of the Midwest was (and probably always will be) among the "flyover states," largely devoid of picture postcard scenery, simply a place to "get through." But when Thomas McGrath, a well-published poet who would become my colleague and close friend in the early seventies, came to Moorhead State, my attitudes began to change. Tom had grown up on a North Dakota farm and delighted in educating me about the region and its history. Exploring my own roots was certainly part of it, too, for both sides of my family were from the region, and reading the midwestern poets such as those Stryk had published was also a major factor. I had known the work of only a few of them, but I came to treasure many, and none more than Ted Kooser, whose sense of the rural Nebraska landscape was truly illuminated through his powerful sense of detail and by the memorable metaphors he was consistently able to find there. As Ted is quoted in Mary K. Stillwell's *The Life & Poetry of Ted Kooser*, he had discovered that his "experiences of living in Iowa and Nebraska were indeed legitimate subjects," the source of his own "Grecian urns." What Ted knew well and what I was slowly learning is what Stryk wrote in the introduction to his first volume:

The Midwest . . . does have characteristic beauty . . . if the poet is worth his salt he is certain to get as much out of it as those who live elsewhere get from mountains and the sea. For what the land does not supply, his imagination will. . . . And if the poets of the heartland see their territory as often luminous and wild, are we to conclude that the weary passer-through who views it as a terrible sameness may, in fact, be seeing nothing other than himself?

I was certainly able to find those ideas in the work of many of the writers in the region, especially those I was to become friends with, including Robert Bly, Linda Hasselstrom, and Bill Holm. But my main influence remained Tom McGrath, who not only encouraged my writing but became the inspiration for the founding of the poetry journal *Dacotah Territory* in 1971. As I became more and more involved as an editor, I also felt the need to write and talk with other editors, to establish "a community of correspondence and publication," as Ted called it. His *New Salt Creek Reader* and publications from Windflower Press inspired me to communicate with him by mail, and, as luck would have it, my family and I were able to detour to Lincoln on our annual summer trip to visit my parents in Kansas, so I could actually meet and talk with Ted—which, thanks to Ted's open and personable nature and willingness to answer my questions and make suggestions, became the beginning of a long friendship.

Something else took place to change my life in the seventies—the founding of Plains Distribution Service, Inc. with my friend, Joe Richardson. In the next five years the organization would distribute much work by midwestern authors and presses via our quarterly book lists and magazine list, and the Plains Bookbus—a large Barth motorhome outfitted as a bookstore, which traveled the region visiting schools and libraries and which sponsored over three hundred readings as well as lectures by midwestern authors. Unfortunately, grant money dried up nationwide in the early eighties, but what an amazing time we had, as our community of correspondence and publication increased immensely. But by

1981 I also found that the proverbial Labor of the Bookbus and the magazine had caught up with the Love—I was simply worn out. But I was very proud of what we'd accomplished in those ten years—of the friends I had made and would keep in touch with, and of everything that had been shared, and published, including Ted's "Shooting a Farmhouse," one of my all-time favorite poems.

As the title of my essay suggests, I'm going to end with one of my own poems, which was first published in the *Midwest Quarterly*'s tribute edition to Ted, in the summer of 2005. The poem was indeed generated by Ted's words in the epigraph, which capture what I consider the major theme of midwestern writing: the discovery and new ways of looking at what's all around us, what's so frequently overlooked. If many of us out here in the flyover zone still write with chips on our shoulders, we also realize that Ted Kooser's selection as both poet laureate and Pulitzer Prize–winner was, in a way, a validation of all of us whose work is grounded in, and who have been shaped by, this "luminous and wild" place.

Great Plains

I delight in the things I discover
right within reach.
—Ted Kooser

Try to think of one more imagination game
to keep you going, maybe what a long, dull
road trip might be compared to—like a job
you hate but need to keep to stay alive.
Or remember the dream you wake from in panic,
the one that won't let go of you for days,
its own tedious roads that keep you looping
back upon yourself. You sing along
with some melody beneath the static.

Try to remember loneliness is supposedly
the beholder's making, even as the sun
slips into heavy clouds it will not
rise from, the dark fields growing into night,
until you notice lights in the distance—
soon startled by bright beams coming at you,
the giant combines churning, the grain trucks
lining up in sheets of billowing dust.

Try to get it down, all of it—the world
within a world you couldn't imagine
till right now—so that when you wake,
finally, you can still feel that dust
beneath your eyelids, the prairie earth
you'll need to pare from fingernails, the
disappearing road still rising up to meet you.

JC REILLY

Bathroom Spiders

for T.K.

They've built a canopy in the old white tub
we don't use, these black house spiders
that moved in some time ago, because they knew,
somehow, they'd live unmolested there.
Carcasses of gnats and small flies collect
on the porcelain beneath the webs,
leftover dinner scraps no one will come by
to pick up, least of all me, in case their removal
should disrupt the spiders' endless spinning
and force a repair job—though, in an old house,
repair jobs seem unavoidable. They've borne
their children there, and grandchildren,
and a few generations besides, always shaking
from their egg sac like prizes from a piñata,
scuttling across the expanse of tub to stake out
a new corner. No more than a few take up
permanent residence in the tub though; perhaps
they find better real estate throughout the house.
For the ones that stay, the accommodations
are spacious if sterile, but their roommates,
blundering as we are, never get in their way.

. . .

To look at Ted is to see a kindly old gentleman who seems down-
to-earth and low-key—not someone to be intimidated by. And yet
I was *terrified* of him when I began taking his tutorial back in my
graduate days at UNL. Terrified of his poetic reputation (which

was staggering twenty years ago and has only blossomed since) and terrified of sharing my lowly work with someone so accomplished. I learned a lot from Ted, about how to see the natural world with an empathetic eye, to find the strange but startling detail that could lift an image beyond itself. I know for a fact he thought most of my poems were somewhere on the continuum between "messy possibilities" and "outright dreck" (he said as much), but he never gave up hope that I would find my own way into poems and poetic seeing. While I still don't presume to be an expert, my poem "Bathroom Spiders," like so many of Ted's poems, takes something mundane and inconsequential and elevates its worth in that magical alchemy of writing we've dedicated so much of our lives to.

When a Place Finds Voice

One of Ted's poems, "Fred Manfred," was written about my father, the Minnesota novelist, Frederick Manfred. After my father died in September of 1994, we held a memorial for him at his home in Luverne, Minnesota. And after the memorial, Ted wrote a marvelous poem about my father's garden. In the poem, Ted speaks of my father's shovel or spade still standing ready for its task in the now abandoned garden, while, of course, the man who made the garden is no longer alive to keep working on it. It's clear in the poem that the man who made the garden was a writer who dedicated himself every day to the garden of words in the form, mostly, of fiction. Ted had driven up from Nebraska for the memorial, and I remember seeing Ted walking around Dad's garden and around Dad's house, observing everything.

That poem Ted wrote about Dad opened a door for me. It reminded me that I, too, had observed my father for many a year, in his garden, in town, by his fireside, and that I, too, could take a look at my notes, or consult my vast constellation of memories, and write a bit more about my father, my friend, at a time when I missed him so deeply. So I wrote several poems about my father for *My Only Home*, a volume of poetry from Red Dragonfly Press, and the two poems I was most happy with were "My Father by the Fire" and "Green Pear Tree in September," a poem that appeared in Ted's weekly column American Life in Poetry.

I've had several discussions with Robert Bly over the years about Ted and Gary Snyder. Robert felt, at the time, that Gary Snyder was probably the greater poet, and I felt that Ted's work was more approachable and powerful. The point is that Robert and I both truly enjoyed the brilliant work of both Snyder and Kooser, and enough with the preferences! Poetry shouldn't be a competition. Each of us can speak of our place in the universe with our own voices. Or, as my father once said, "If a 'place' truly finds voice, at last the ultimate sacred force speaks." That statement is true when it comes to Ted Kooser—the sacred force of Nebraska and of America is speaking in Ted's lifelong work.

Writing toward Home

I first met Ted Kooser when I was twenty-five, as a graduate student attending a small liberal arts college located on the banks of the Red River in Minnesota. *Delights & Shadows* had just won the Pulitzer Prize for Poetry, and, as the current U.S. Poet Laureate, Ted was traveling the country, reading and discussing poetry to a wide general audience. It has been said that Ted presented at and visited more places for the cause of poetry than any other poet laureate.

What I remember from Ted's visit is his gentle voice, accessible poems, and the care and patience he offered the audience. After the reading, he sat at a small table outside of the auditorium to sign books and briefly interact with people. I must have waited almost forty-five minutes to reach the front of the line and hand him my copy of *Delights & Shadows* to sign. The auditorium had been packed full of people earlier, and the line extended down the hall and through the building doors to outside on the campus lawn. Even so, Ted didn't turn anyone away nor did he stop signing books until the crowd dissipated and everyone else went home for the night.

If you told me that one day Ted Kooser would be my teacher, I wouldn't have believed you. Not for a second. But life has a funny way of working itself out, and our paths *did* cross again five years later—either by fate, hard work, or just sheer luck.

In the fall of 2009—my second year as a PhD student in English at UNL—I enrolled in Ted's poetry tutorial. For the first few weeks of class, I brought drafts of poems that tried too hard: flashy poems that experimented with language or performed stylistic acrobatics to grab readers' attention. Looking back, I realize many of these drafts were weak imitations of other poems—poor attempts to impress classmates and readers. The emotion and subject matter of these poems often rang hollow and untrue, and Ted sensed it right away.

He probably also sensed that I was struggling, like many students, to find my voice and confidence as a writer. Instead of stating what wasn't working in my drafts, Ted showed me compassion and kindness. He asked questions to learn more about me—about where I was from, my family, and my interests. I shared a bit about my life growing up in the Northwest Angle and Islands of Lake of the Woods, about fishing, about how much I missed the Northwoods, lakes, and snow since moving to Nebraska. And Ted shared stories about his travels to Minnesota and talked about some of his writer friends there. I could have easily sat in his office for hours just listening to his stories.

At the end of one tutorial session, he gave me a couple of books written by Minnesota poets whom we both admired. Through this kind gesture, Ted gave me more than just poetry books. He gave me the confidence and guidance to write about the place where I am from and share it with readers, even if others may think that such places or subjects are not interesting, popular, or in literary fashion. He reminded me that one poem may change a reader's perception of the place and give them a new way to see the world.

Instead of being embarrassed and writing *away from* my home-place, I started writing *toward* it. The following weeks I wrote and brought Ted poems about island life and fishing, poems about trees and birds, and poems about blizzards, snow, and ice. By incorporating my observations, experiences, and concrete images of the natural world, my poems rang more authentic and truer than my previous writing. I was slowly honing my voice as a poet. "Lake of the Woods" is one such poem I wrote in Ted's tutorial course. The poem became the heartbeat of my creative dissertation, which later evolved into my debut poetry collection, *Now/Here*. Without Ted's insight and guidance, I'm not sure if the poem or manuscript would have come into being.

Lake of the Woods

I've gazed at the same sky and same ceiling
of stars from the same dock wondering
what I want from life, and perhaps, if I had not
left so soon, so many years ago, but stayed here,
by now I would have trained my eyes to recognize
what I was seeking—the barbs on the vane
of a pinion feather, muskrats resting in elegant reeds,
the diaspora of pine cones under the trees.

JONATHAN GREENE

One Light to Another

The storm
turns off
the lights.

The lightning
lights the whereabouts
of the flashlight.

The flashlight
takes us to matches
and candles, the oil lamp.

Now we're back,
revisiting
the 19th century.

. . .

I have known Ted a long time. Perhaps more than twenty years. We have many mutual friends and have published each other's work. This poem was reprinted in Ted's weekly American Life in Poetry, Column 489. Also, we have visited each other's homes (Nebraska and Kentucky), and Ted and Kathy came to an art show I had with my wife, Dobree Adams, in Missouri in 2009.

DAN GERBER

In Praise of Ted Kooser

I've known Ted since our first correspondence in the late sixties, about some poems for Windflower Press, and then, until 2016, as one actor in a three-way correspondence with Jim Harrison and me, often several exchanges a week for almost two decades. And it was a decade into that often-rousing conversation that I actually met Ted face-to-face when, during his laureateship, he came to read at the University of California at Santa Barbara, and we met as old friends.

It wouldn't be at all a surprise to select the predominate emotion evoked by Ted Kooser's poems as kindness, not just the simple kindness of an elderly couple "splitting an order," though that too, but the elemental kindness of close looking, of seeing and framing for us the vividness of the most ordinary experience we, through habit, busyness, greed, or indifference, edit out of our lives. Whatever the source of our inattention, it leaves a wound; it leaves a sense of poverty in our spirits, and I think it's the particular genius of Ted's art to sense those vulnerable places and to create the nearly perfect balm to make us whole again, even for a moment, to make us care to see the world we've hurried through again and to see it, and ourselves, in a kinder light.

TODD DAVIS

Fishing with Nightcrawlers

Ames, Iowa

From the bank beneath a basswood, I fling a nightcrawler
for my sons, too small to cast for themselves. The bait drifts
with the current, and I pass the rod to the oldest one,
my own hands secretly holding from below.
You were a boy in this town along the South Skunk River.
I wonder if you carried your pole over your left
or right shoulder, if the worms you dug in the backyard,
squirming as you lowered them over the hook, smelled
on your fingers when you handed the bluegill you caught
to your mother, the stringer clanking against the sink's
enamel basin. Her fingers filmed over as she dunked
the meat in egg and milk, rolled the pink flesh
in breadcrumbs, the kitchen hazy with burnt butter,
as if a boy in vestments had trailed by the table
swinging a censer, how you peered through the hole
made by her elbow and waist, hoping there'd be enough
white bread to sop up the blackened grease.

. . .

I first read Ted Kooser's poems while living in DeKalb, Illinois, in 1989. I was a young graduate student at Northern Illinois University in a class taught by the Zen Buddhist poet Lucien Stryk, who had edited *Heartland II: Poets of the Midwest* and included some of Ted's work in that volume.

I was especially drawn to "I Put My Hand on His Head" and "Phoning My Son Long Distance," two poems about Ted's relationship with his son after the divorce. More than thirty years later, I still return to these lines and their startling images as I think of my own sons:

His skull is heavy and sun-warmed—
a stone from a lost field,

an unopened geode,
crowded with beautiful crystals.

When I was twenty-six, Ted's poetry showed me a way forward, an unexpected path because I had no plans of becoming a poet. His work, over the years, in all its manifestations (including his paintings), has meant so much and continued to serve as a guide and a testament.

"Fishing with Nightcrawlers" was born out of the year I lived in Ames with my wife and two boys, serving as visiting poet-in-residence at Iowa State University in 2002.

In the evenings, I often found myself wandering the town, thinking about Ted—What might he have noticed as he walked this block? Did he know this basswood tree, the three trunks grown large together?—and as a poet with only one book at the time, I hoped some small bit of what made Ted such a great poet might rub off on me and help me write more poems, poems that would matter in someone else's life as Ted's poems mattered in mine.

House

Ghosts in the attic.
Heaven made of foam.

Pink insulation
unfurling like a gown.

      The (sad) glitter of it.

My love of decay
ever frothing.

Dribbling stucco
witness to the rain.

Sodden soffits.
The wood gone soft.

Slope-shouldered
doorways

      perfectly askew.

Broken down
penny tile like a whole

      mess of bad teeth.

Windows fractured by stars.

Some days only
a squirrel walked by.

Some days only clouds.

Each space occupied
by its dream.

All I ever wanted
was a porch

    I could die on

and a swing whose breeze
would carry me.

. . .

One of Ted's many gifts was his ability to create community
beyond our class tutorials. I fondly remember how, in the first
year of my PhD program at UNL, he invited a group of graduate
students out to his farm for a bonfire with readings, popcorn,
and new friends. I'm also grateful for his lessons on metaphor
and compression in poetry, which still inform my own writing
and teaching. It was an honor to read with him at the Sunken
Garden Poetry Festival (Farmington, Connecticut) in June 2015.

SANDRA YANNONE

A Valentine Sonnet

for Ted Kooser

From his writing studio every winter in Garland,
he crafted valentines. And every February 14th
or thereabouts, I'd find one delivered by hand,
on its hearty card stock, tucked beneath

heaps of late student papers and policy-imbued
memos in my English department mailbox. Twenty years
now with Lincoln and Andrews Hall in my rear-view
mirror, I often misremember Ted's hometown, swear

to my friends that yes, indeed, this U.S. poet
laureate lived on a farm in a town named
Valentine, where each August, I'd drive out
for the annual corn and beer. And who could blame

me? Who doesn't want to know a carrier from Valentine,
gifting poems to the world, the beloved and divine?

JOYCE SUTPHEN

At the Graveyard

I discover my name,
though I will never
be buried here, next to
my parents (when they die)
and my sister (who died years ago).

It's hot, and the grass is stiff
as we cross from my sister
to where my grandparents
are buried, surrounded by
townspeople of another time.

I had thought it would be sad
to wander these paths with my parents,
but we're cheerful this afternoon,
comparing marker styles and letterings,
connecting headstones with faces we remember.

In fact, they seem more at home here than
they were at the place we just left—
a store filled with pillows and fountains, copper
pots and pans, peppermills and jars of jam and
salsa, lanterns, lamps and upholstered chairs.

"And what would we do with any of this?" my father
said, shaking his head in wonderment.

. . .

Ted Kooser's poems are as natural and true as anything I know in American poetry. I love his honed-down style, his subtle humor, and his attention to a detail that will shine with kindness and grace by the end of the poem. That's exactly what I try to do in my poems.

Grace in Poetry

I first "met" Ted in his *Winter Morning Walks: 100 Postcards to Jim Harrison,* reading and rereading the profound poems in the quiet of my own early mornings, ironically wrapped in a warm blanket. One benefit of reading is that we can drive forward in reverse, and I then sought his earlier work. Like so many others, I anticipated his upcoming publications, deeply touched and renewed by the lyrical descriptions and the sense of mystery inside the smallest details. In the spring of 2004, the same year that Ted was named U.S. Poet Laureate, I was fortunate to take his poetry class at the University of Nebraska. North light streamed in the large windows of that ground-floor classroom of Andrews Hall. Chairs were arranged in a half circle, and Ted sat at the front of the room. He introduced his own poetry journey, his work as an insurance company executive, rising early to write before work, and his approach to the specific. He made the writing of poetry seem possible in various life circumstances, and he made our own poetry significant with his thoughtful consideration and close examination of how our poems were structured.

I am still applying and making discoveries from what I learned that semester, and I continue to be amazed by his generosity of time, knowledge, and encouragement, both in the classroom and in outside meetings. An example is the March 22 extended email response from Ted on "some thoughts about your poem." He discusses the title, why it leads in one direction while the poem diverges onto another topic, and he suggests a slight alteration. He then analyzes the poem line-by-line and by stanza, including sounds, line breaks, details of imagery, connecting the logic of those images and editing unnecessary complications. His detailed commentary on this poem has continued, more than fifteen years later, to serve as a personal guide to revising and refining my current poems. He ends the email with a paragraph on a discussion we had about "voice," posing questions to ask myself about accessibility and clarity for the reader.

I continue to learn from Ted's new writings, his books on the craft, and his promotion of poetry. Each Sunday, I scan the newspaper headlines of a world that sometimes seems to careen off its axis, then I arrive at my destination, his weekly column, American Life in Poetry. In the midst of the news on chaos and strife, Ted offers a reflective pause, a moment of clarity, an affirmation of grace in poetry and the everyday life.

Making Ice Angels

Dry winter. Yesterday, I turned on the sprinklers.

Into the star-speckled night, a full moon sailed inside two
   halos.

I dreamt lifetimes rolling up out of water, oozing from mud,
. . . ghost . . . gills . . . fish . . . reptile . . . feather.
I woke to a sparrow tapping on the frosted window.

Nine inches coat today in quiet. Soft and comforting. Soup,
bread. Daffodils believing in the protective walls around us,
we give up sacrificing our time—
we pare down to the bone.

I tell the mandevilla plants I'm sorry.
Plunging into winter spaces, I lug them from the cluttered
hallway onto the patio. They know the dust and canker
of the body, the way crystals form in the cold.

The neighbors break through the unmarked shawl,
stomp paths over their porch, across their yard. Muffled
voices of smoke, they rumble away in chilly cars.

Elbows of bare viburnum branches rub in a swirling gust;
milky clumps plump down hieroglyphs.

Shoveling, my fingers stiffen inside mittens.
I imagine animals sharing heat, burrowed
inside a thousand underground rooms.

The shovel's metal lip rasps against concrete
as I scrape and lift, scrape and lift,
amassing hills
of luminous white.

Making Sense, Making a Life

Ted Kooser, even before I knew him, was present at major mile-stones in my life. I first met Ted through his poem "Urine Speci-men," which I read as an undergraduate. I felt a strange solidarity with the simple way he recorded this mundane collection, since I had just been diagnosed with kidney stones; this required me to collect a twenty-four-hour sample of my own, which I stored in my dormmate's minifridge until walking it to my follow-up appointment in a brown paper bag.

Years later, after a fair amount of twenty-something drifting, I didn't know what I wanted to be. I knew I wanted to write poems and that I wanted them to feel real and lived. I enrolled in a Master of Fine Arts program. I met the other poets in my first workshop. Clockwise around the room we each shared our names, homes, and poets whose work we admired. A stranger and I both spoke our names, then Ted's name. Something came into focus.

Those MFA years brought discovery after discovery. I couldn't read or write or live fast enough. I aimed everything at finishing my degree. In my final semester, as I narrowed in on that goal, I began to feel anchorless again. My manuscript adviser, like a flash of light-ning, shocked me out of my tunnel vision. Graduation wasn't time to stop studying. I needed more. Maybe I would apply for PhD pro-grams. First on my list was Nebraska. Maybe I could study with Ted.

I met Ted on April 25, 2012. It was his seventy-third birthday. I had been offered a place at the University of Nebraska and had flown in to decide if I would accept. The previous year had been so full of stress and uncertainty that actually being there in Nebraska felt surreal. I met with Ted in his office for what would be the first of many meetings. I don't remember what we talked about. I do remember the big, upholstered chair by his desk.

I remember the two of us sat next to each other for a reading downstairs. We ate cookies from a catering tray. I could hear him chewing. The Pulitzer Prize–winner and former U.S. Poet Laureate had come to campus to meet me on his birthday, and here we were quietly eating cookies like nothing about this was weird.

That summer I drove myself the 1,800 miles from Vermont to Nebraska. It's hard to overstate how much of an upheaval this was. It felt unreal, like I was living an idea instead of a life. In my first tutorial session with Ted, I brought him a poem that in retrospect I know was laughably unready and trying too hard to be everything I thought a poem should be. I showed up with the grandiose hopefulness of a pilgrim seeking wisdom from an oracle. Ted rightly but gently took that poem down a few notches, and this was my first lesson with him about distinguishing a poem's idea from its reality. It wasn't enough for me to wish my poems into being; I had to really do the work of making them, of putting them into form and context. I also had to stop seeing Ted as a Pulitzer Prize–winner at a distance and start seeing him as the guy wearing a cable knit sweater who brought the biggest box of Whitman's Sampler chocolates I've ever seen to the department holiday party. I had to look at myself differently, too. I had to stop seeing myself as an ignorant outsider with raging imposter syndrome and instead show up to the work of reinventing myself and my poems. I had to see that Ted and I were both people, both poets trying all the time to listen better and write better.

Ted taught me that it's not enough for a poet to have a creative imagination. For a poem to feel real and lived, it always has to make sense—this is not as simple as it sounds. A poem has to build its own logic that holds true to how we know the world. Its wildness needs to be grounded in observation, in detail, in connection, in trying to understand. On second thought, maybe it is that simple; the way you build a poem is like the way you build yourself—through attention, through listening, through remembering the moments that make you.

Time's Beard, His Closest Thing to Seasons

He shaves it each spring so it grows back like the earth.
But first there's the grooming. He pulls a bone comb
from the cabinet—the one with little fish
etched on the handle—and sets them swimming through
    his beard.
It's a steady ritual, like tending a field, like mending old
    shoes.

We are, each in our brief surprise, the loose bits that fall to
    the sink.
Wood shavings, flaked varnish, cinnamon swirling toward
    the drain,
watery comets streaking on their way out.

His hound ambles through the hall like a kind of mountain,
steady claws dragging along the hardwood.
Suddenly there's a wet nose at the back of Time's knee
He remembers he's forgotten the whiskey
and goes to pull the bottle from its high kitchen shelf.
It's an even pour, amber filling the cup's lake bottom
half full and shimmering. You'd almost think
birds and frogs lived there, their bodies searching for sun.

Back in the bathroom, Time waits a while at the mirror,
reading a map of his face that doesn't change,
then toasts himself, swallows it all down,
and brings the razor to his jaw,
hair coming down like shedding leaves.

How I Found Ted

In 1996, shortly after my family and I moved to the Garland area, I followed an arrow to a garage sale by Branched Oak Lake. There, I found a paperweight with a black-and-white photo of William Jennings Bryan's home in Lincoln, Nebraska. As I was paying, I told the man working that this was the home my mom was housed in for nursing school in 1953 and that it was going to make the perfect Mother's Day gift. He replied, "Wait a minute," and disappeared out the side door. After quite a while he came back with a print of a painting he'd done of a small-town neighborhood block, each home with a quilt hanging over the porch rail. "Something I painted for my mother," he said, and asked that I give it to my mom. I returned the next day with more money, but the man wasn't there; instead, a friend of his from Colorado was working the sale. I inquired about the man, mentioning how kind he was and what he gave me. She told me that he was quite well known, Ted Kooser: "You can look him up." I pulled out of the driveway and headed straight to the Seward library, checking out all of his books. I ran into Ted again at the Mill in the Haymarket in Lincoln. He remembered me from his garage sale, and since then our paths continued to cross.

I was there when Ted walked my friend, Denise Banker, outside to show her the rainbow after the wake for her husband, Bill Yates, at the Beaver Bakery in Beaver Crossing. They stood side-by-side with their arms around each other long enough that the image is seared into my head. When my daughter, Allie, was writing a report on the blizzard of 1888, Ted and his wife, Kathy, offered to show her the tombstone at the Seward Cemetery of the schoolteacher who had died in the storm.

Ted wrote my letter of recommendation in 2008 for my Master of Fine Arts degree at the University of Nebraska–Omaha. I remember being terrified when I handed Ted ten of my poems—terrified, because I wasn't an English major, because I was forty-five, and because the only class I'd ever taken was Creative Writing at Platte College in 1982. I found out years later the class was taught by one of Ted's colleagues, Emily Uzendoski. Ted not only wrote my letter of recommendation but also sent me a copy of the letter (which I had not asked for), and I kept the letter on my wall next to my writing desk as a way to keep momentum through my MFA program, and beyond.

Ted is the kind of person who, when I asked him if he'd give me some feedback on the order of my poems in my manuscript, would return them with a typed-out critique of where I'd gone astray and written comments on each individual poem—teaching me new ways to look at my writing when ready to revise and publish. He is kind.

Tuesdays with Ted Kooser: How I Found the Heart behind My Collection of Poems, *Pulse*

When I turned in my unpublished manuscript of poems, Ted didn't mince words.

> Dear Maria,
>
> You're wearing a mask of toughness, and I suspect it's feeling a little hot on your face. We've talked about vulnerability, and we can both agree that there's a tender, caring Maria beneath all these poems, but as of now, I don't see it.
>
> I'm not saying we need to fall all over ourselves being likable. Still, the speaker throughout these poems is constantly judging everyone, and nobody wants to spend a lot of time with someone who is always judging others— even when they need judging!

When I used to sell sunglasses, I'd put on a pair with amber lenses when I was bored. Everything came to life: the sunglasses, trapped in cases of glass like pinned butterflies, popped with color. The plants in the corner glowed space-alien green.

As I looked through my draft, Ted's words sharpened into focus. My speaker looked like a real asshole. Was that the way I wanted people to remember me? In one poem, "Tits and Violin," the speaker describes an encounter:

> When a guy in the bar says he loves nothing more than tits
>   and violin, and I don't punch him,
> I know I've mellowed with time like a fading chord.

This hostility coated the manuscript like a lime deposit. For the first time, I saw myself as Ted or a distant reader would: as someone whose tragically tough veneer allows zero room for vulnerability.

That persona, moreover, clashes with my personality. I'm no wimp, but I despise conflict. When interacting with other people, I give the benefit of the doubt until proven otherwise. I over-trust, override my good sense—and boy, have I paid dearly for that. I've got a destructive streak and a broken urge to make people who hate my guts fall in love with me. And aren't these the more interesting issues that I ought to explore?

This person was absent throughout the collection: and my authentic self is kinder, more compelling than that harsh voice.

So, I took off the mask, put on amber lenses, and focused on more interesting questions: Why do we love friends who are pains-in-the-asses, especially when they wake us up to borrow our car? Why do people love us, when we're such flawed humans?

As I considered these questions, my collection reshaped itself. The tenor throughout the poems has shifted. If you'll look at "The Ghost's Daughter Speaks," this poem still retains that energy I'd worried about losing if my voice softened but acknowledges the flawed relationship that the speaker has with her mother.

Yet, the content and the poem are primarily about forgiveness, communication problems, and how we can meet each other halfway, even in a damaged relationship.

Almost all of my poems within the last few years speak to Ted's feedback. I chose "The Ghost's Daughter Speaks" for this volume because, according to the poem's creation date, I would have written the poem soon after Ted and I had that exchange.

The speaker in this poem neither shames nor demonizes her subject; instead, she creates an awkward, broken halfway point. There isn't a mask of toughness; in fact, the speaker discusses how, although she is banishing the ghosts of perfection, she'll strive to meet the subject halfway, even though they may never walk through the walls that separate them.

So, amid our mad dash to publish and add cv lines, I ask myself this: Does this manuscript do justice to my voice? Do these poems resonate with likability?

Although we don't want our speaker to represent us, we assume responsibility when we inhabit that first person. Whether we like it or not, our reader assesses our likability, and those perceptions inform whether or not she turns the page.

Regardless of what happens to this speaker, I know what happens in this poem: this narrator is neither beige wallflower nor whiskey-chugging cliché. Instead, she stumbles blindly through tragedy and joy and leads the reader (and herself) with compassion. For this, I am grateful for those many Tuesdays spent with Ted.

The Ghost's Daughter Speaks

I'm giving up the other ghosts of shame that rise when someone
hands me love's glass apple. And the ghost of a girl

who stalks childhood halls on a hot Midwestern evening, who,
around happy hour feels a tug

of sadness when her mother's eyes darken and say, this mess
is your fault, I'm giving that up, too.

I'm giving up the idea that I can clean every mess or run from it,
so that we can begin, clean,

as rain cutting a windshield. On that night when my grandmother
was dying, and we pulled over, and my mother talked me

down from a torrent of grief, I choose to see that and banish
demons of blame like cigarettes

I've never smoked but traded for a different addiction: for you
to tell me I'm enough. I'm giving up perfect

in exchange for good enough: Like when the man I've known
for only a week awakens at 5 AM to hand me a cup of coffee.

I'm giving up the notion that joy is a red-roped club through
which only the elite can pass, that love is a locked door

against which I throw myself. I give up waiting to be told
what I can and can't say: stranded on the tarmac

of silence. Refuse to stand at the bus station of hope, too scared
to buy a ticket that could take me

somewhere else. Let's take this somewhere else, beyond our
bodies' crippled attempts to talk. Meet me halfway

before the burning bridges of resentment, after rivers that
forget, beyond this house where words

fail us. Let's walk through walls of grief. If we can't get through,
let's press our ears against them and strain, forever, to listen.

Mercurius

HER COLLAR

Sometimes at night it winks at me. The light haunting. I watch it and imagine all the ways it can be killed. When she's in deep sleep, eyelids restless with dreams, the way mine do, if she had a tail it would be thumping, that's when I go to work on the thing around her ankle. I've tried chewing the hard plastic, the metal, but my teeth keep sliding off. The softer part made of collar material like mine but thicker. It gives in my mouth, but it's too tight to get a grip on so I lick and lick to soften it like I do strips of rawhide she gives me. And maybe a shoe once in a while. When I manage to snag a tooth and tug, that light blinks furiously and I know I'm in trouble.

Her leg twitches like she's wearing the shock collar my old person used to make me wear—don't get me started on that though. I belly crawl off the side of the bed, knowing I'm exiled to the floor now. I always have to ask permission for her bed. It's a night of working on my posture then, getting my back aligned straight, my ribs and hips in perfect order on the wood floor, next to her slippers I love so much. I take the place her heel rests in my mouth and chew the soft lamb's wool just a little for comfort as I fall asleep. I don't think she even notices.

1/2 AN HOUR A DAY

That's how long my walk is. Or two times at fifteen minutes. Pee poop stretch the legs smell every other dog, child, squirrel, rabbit, rat, big human bicycle: all in fifteen minutes. I go home and collapse afterwards, my ass sore from pushing so hard. Color rubbed off my nose. It's lost its respectable black. Now it's mottled red brown like a Brittany Spaniel. God do I hate those guys. So nervous they pee if you even look twice at them. Their hearts humming like the old refrigerator in her apartment. It needs the dust cleaned off the coils! I try to tell her every way I can think of, but good luck. She didn't even bother to argue for longer walks. Just look at my legs, the deep chest, the shoulders—I'm made to run! I must have retriever blood! Even though I'm a Corgi. I beat the Greyhound at the dog park we used to go to. Not anymore. No. It's fifteen minutes away and she doesn't want the other two-legs to know about her ankle collar.

HOW THE CAR RIDES STOPPED

It was all her fault. At first I misunderstood. Thought she'd run down a pack of dogs and I was ready to chew her arm off. No, I heard her explain to her mother, she might have been drinking from the bad bottle that made my stomach hurt and came shooting out the other end when I lapped up the puddle she spilled on the floor. Also, what I saw was her hand full of white pills—for worms or what I get after I eat raccoon poop and my stomach is full of worms wanting me to eat more and more—She doesn't tell her mom about the worm pills. I was lucky she left me at home that night. She was crazy. Talking and complaining under her breath like an old dog having to get up and move out of the doorway. She was just looking for a fight. I've seen her like that before.

I went a while thinking she'd driven her car into a pack of beach dogs, like I said, and even though I didn't know them, they were my kind and I stayed mad at her for a while. Ate holes in her soft blanket I liked so much it hurt me too. Then one day her friend Tooey came over bringing medicine that made them romp around like puppies and I couldn't help myself— all that joy! I barked and play nipped and lapped up the pieces of popcorn when she poured the bowl over her friend Tooey's head. No butter. She was trying to keep her legs and arms sapling thin, but I liked it.

When she told the story of her night car ride on the beach again, it was three women! Not dogs! She tried to run down! I loved her so much I worked extra hard on the ankle collar that night, chipping a tooth, but the pain went away in a few days. We'd have to find another way. What a meal for the beach dogs, I dreamed. I shuddered at the pieces of fat and muscle and gristle and bone flying through the air, stuck on the car's front grill. They'd be sick for sure with all that fresh meat—

MEALTIME

She says we both need to eat less, which is sad news to me, as she fills my bowl with carrots and peas (I hate peas and always leave the little grey green knobs in the freshly licked bowl), beans and broccoli. I know the names because she holds them up and says it over and over until I bark "got it!" in my language. Instead of chicken or beef or lamb or my favorite salmon, she drops a mound of brown rice on top of the vegies. It's better than white rice, she says, we can live on the same food now. You can have my leftovers. I perk up at that idea, but then realize that only means more rice and vegetables, probably peas. I bet she doesn't like them either.

But she's the happiest I've seen her since she got back from the bad place that made her clothes so ugly she threw them in the trash. I had to dig them out that night and drag them to the corner of the screened porch behind the sofa where I hide my special finds, like her clothes from prison, the hooskow, she called it. I've been in jail, caged when they caught me running free and living homeless. I had friends, but that's another story— She paid "good money" to spring me, she told her friend Tooey. So now I owe her.

It's quieter here, I'll give her that. Except for nights she goes crazy and turns the music so loud I howl against my ear pain until she turns it down. She dances and jumps around, and I notice how the ankle with the collar isn't as graceful. It lags behind like she's got a thorn in her paw, or somebody stepped on it. I feel bad for her and jump around too to keep her from noticing her injury. I just don't want her to get sad again and I have to do my business on the hall rug because she won't get out of bed no matter how hard I bark and pull at the blanket she has over her head. She takes the worm pills those sad times, but not in cream cheese like I need when I eat the raccoon poop and have to see the vet.

Every time we go I think to myself, okay, this is it, The Big Goodbye, and I cry and snuggle and look deep in her eyes to show I'm sorry for whatever I've done. But that's never it. And after each visit, we go and get ice cream! Not now though, now she barely has time to walk me around the block for a quick pee or two. I remind myself not to drink too much water, like I did when she went out for hours and hours and drove the car into the bushes or the mailbox at dawn.

Yesterday, a man came to the door and she gave him the keys and he drove the car away! I was terribly sad and already missing the smoked knuckle bone I'd tucked away in the back seat where I usually stood with my head out the window. I could still see where I licked the glass waiting for her to come out of the grocery store where she bought me cans of beef, chicken, lamb and my favorite, salmon . . . before we started eating the same food.

WHAT SHE DOES ALL DAY

At first she used pencils that made colors on the paper. I ate a blue one and turned my tongue that scary color the Shar Pei at the dog park showed us one day. It was truly awful, plus that droopy skin, we all ran away as fast as we could, leaving the stick we'd been playing with so he could strut around like he invented trees or something afterwards. I always avoided him. A real monster. She frowned and didn't think it was funny or sad that my tongue was blue, and I couldn't get outside to eat grass and clean things up. When I lapped from the toilet, the water turned blue and

I thought, oh no, she's going to know I've been lapping from the toilet again. But she didn't say anything. She was too busy putting colors on the paper.

I tried to see what she was making, but it wasn't clear until she switched to paint her mom brought her in a big bag of tubes and brushes and these squares of white. They hugged and laughed, and her mom scratched my head, something she's never done.

Only nine more months, her mom said and glanced at the ankle collar. I shivered. That sounded like forever.

I sighed and went to the porch and laid down behind the sofa with my head on the pile of my things. I'd added a pair of her underpants last night, and the scent smelled good, though not as rich as when she was still eating meat. And I remembered the shore dogs and the splattering bodies of the three women. They hadn't even been touched, as it turned out, just frightened. She told Tooey that the women said she didn't even try to brake or slow down and they had to jump out of the way.

What did they expect, she said, they were on my beach at three in the morning! She laughed and shook her head. I have nothing to say here. If I see someone, my kind or another, on the sidewalk in front of our apartment, I tear the roof off trying to get to them. I have to respect that kind of watchfulness.

Anyway, putting color on a brush and plastering it on the white cloth makes her happy, so I am too. When she finally holds up a painting to show me, I smile and wag my tail really hard, thinking maybe she'll fetch me one of the jerky treats her mom left for me. But she doesn't. She starts another picture. It takes a few days for me to realize that what she's painting are lilies. She tells me this so I know. Single ones, whole fields, etched on walls, growing out of a dog's skull . . . is that me? I go to lick the picture to see and she snatches it away. She begins to paint more dogs and lilies. I have them growing out of my ears, my back, my four legs, and my ass.

Put the Shar Pei in one, I try to tell her using my deep-looking eyes, but she doesn't get it. How about the Brittany or that yappy

Cairn Terrier with the crusty eyes that lives upstairs? I keep sending her messages, but she's not receiving. She paints a picture of a dog at a bowl of lilies instead of food, and I grow uneasy. She uses reds and yellows and blues, but her favorite is white. Soon there are pictures of onions and asparagus . . . both unfortunate adventures in eating. I can hardly stand to walk past those pictures lining the hallway wall to dry.

Time's going fast now, she says to me on our morning walk. Hurry up! I'm practically dribbling pee down my legs as she rushes me along.

SMOKE AND FIRE

I smelled the smoke for days before her mom called to tell her about the wildfire. It kept me up most nights, watching the ceiling for the flickering light that would mean the fire was closing in on us. I paced to the living room and looked out the front of the building and tried to get the other animals to tell me the news. They were still mad at the way I chased them and ate their poop though. I moaned loud enough for the Cairn Terrier upstairs to answer, and we made a truce and said we'd bark if we saw fire close.

We went on even faster walks in the smoke days, but we didn't dare walk too fast because it made our lungs hurt and our eyes sting. I think she would have liked it if I refused to leave the house, lifted a leg in the hallway instead. I had to go out there though. I had to see and smell and hear. Was the sidewalk hotter to the touch? Was the fire coming from below us? When the wind blew ash into our faces, I knew it wouldn't be long. The ash was from the stand of pine trees by the dog park and I hated the idea of those trees burning down. It would be too hot there and we'd have no sticks to drag around. I wondered what the Shar Pei was up to with his blue tongue. Maybe it wasn't such a bad thing, the blue tongue.

We were back inside gulping water in ten minutes. She wet a washcloth and put it over her face and stood there breathing the moist air in and out like a panting dog. Then she wet it again and put it over my nose and eyes and I liked how the air smelled like water instead of fire. She gave me a jerky treat and smiled at me, and I knew we were in this together.

Should we evacuate? she asked me. I didn't know the word! I felt the panic rise from my toes up my belly and along my ribs. I shook my head, letting my ears clap loudly enough to drown out my fear.

I don't think so either, she said with a curious little smile. She gave me a second jerky though I hadn't eaten the first one and went to the dining room where she had set up her easel and paints. On the stand was an empty canvas.

She squeezed a tube of white and another of yellow and picked up her brush. A lily appeared floating in the air. She squeezed a dab of red next to the yellow, and then black and brown. I'd never seen her use these colors together. I'm a black and brown and white Corgi, and when she painted me, the colors were always exact. Now the lily was coming out of brown and black earth—a fire burned around it in red and yellow! The center of the lily held a face, it was a woman person, like her! The lily grew and the fire raged, and I worried that it wasn't only in the painting.

I thought I could smell thicker smoke and there was crackling like wood burning and I listened for the upstairs dog to warn me, and I whirled away to check the windows, and outside it was thick gray like she'd painted it, and I couldn't even see the sidewalk! I barked as loud as I could, listened for the Cairn but there was only silence. Then a long bleating horn, signaling over and over! We had to get out of there!

I ran back to her, but she was on the floor, cutting away the ankle collar with a big knife she used to slice a chicken in half. The collar blinked and began to wail and when she was done, she laughed, and stood, and beckoned for me to follow, the cuts on her ankle where the knife slipped, dripping down onto the floor, leaving flower shaped prints for me to follow as if she were the God who made the fire, made me, made it all.

. . .

For several years, Ted and I both lived outside Lincoln and shared stories about the wonderful antics of our dogs. I felt like they were an extension of our friendship and provided humor and joy to our lives. Later, Ted wrote "Death of a Dog," the best, most moving poem I have ever read when his last dog passed away. He so accurately caught the place they hold in our houses and our hearts that it makes me weep to read it again. So this story is for Ted with thanks for capturing so perfectly how we come to love and to know love through our furry friends.

MATT MASON

Opening Night Rehearsal

Tonight, I am the stand-in for Ted Kooser
as they test the new auditorium's new spotlight on my shape.

I read notes
into the new microphone
while the director sits with a stopwatch,

he looks like a swimmer bobbing in a sea of seats.
When I finish, I will wade out there,
the symphony playing as if just for me,

and I will pull out a pen, unfold some paper
and write a poem as, right now,
I'm Poet Laureate of the United States.

Who would waste such a doorway
they're permitted to squeeze through,
asked to slip on the one suit jacket that

almost fits, look up to the celebrated opera singer
smiling at them before the steady launch her voice
fires to the edges of atmosphere.

JUDITH HARRIS

For Ted, On His Hiatus

This morning, just before dawn,
the moon still bright as a key
that fits any lock, I think of you
throwing on the lights from
room to room, your day
planned out for working with
your hands, sawing wood planks
or doing odd jobs you've been
meaning to do, or maybe picking
kale or cucumbers from
Kathy's garden, or plugging up
holes the woodchuck dug
on the dirt floor of the barn,
the sweetness of hay filling your
nostrils, and on your way back,
you tell me that you catch
a rare glimpse of a doe shuttling
her newborn between legs,
and watch as she nibbles leaves
off low hanging branches,
offering the fawn what she can.

Ready to Hold My Hand: Ted Kooser
as Mentor and Friend

Each time I teach a creative writing course, or talk to students individually about their poetry, I hear myself saying,

> You need to be on the lookout for what others fail to notice—the incongruous detail. Keep a notebook or use your phone to keep track of these things. When you are able to weave one of those details into a poem, it is like a bit of neon that brings the text to life. As Williams famously said, "No ideas but in things." So, keep a mental toolbox of things you collect; you will find it incredibly useful.

Each time I say it, I think of Ted Kooser because he always challenged me to make use of the everyday details that surround me, the ones that escape the conscious attention of most people.

In "At the St. Elizabeth Mammography Center," I use the dregs of coffee to illuminate the sense of time and place—to emphasize the uneasy feeling of being in a hospital waiting room. The focus on the cup of coffee is important because, while a cup of coffee is a detail familiar in everyday twenty-first-century life, this isn't just any cup of coffee. This is not the cup of morning coffee you drink from a favorite mug in your kitchen or the ubiquitous Starbucks to-go cup. This flimsy and uninviting cup is definitely not what you would have if you were somewhere you actually wanted to be. The relief of disposing of it parallels the relief of departing the hospital.

As it happens, this poem is autobiographical, and while he always hates when I tell this story, it was Ted who accompanied me (at the time, I was still one of his graduate students) to the hospital for a follow-up mammogram. We had a meeting earlier that day, and he noticed I was distracted, so he asked me why. Nearly two decades later, I am still enormously grateful that he was there, because if the news had been bad, I cannot imagine how I would have managed alone.

And, yes, it was well beyond his responsibility to me as a teacher, but his spontaneous decision to join me that afternoon was also a lesson I have carried into every meeting I have had with students over the years. Sometimes what is called for is not what my students or I might have imagined. Teaching, especially in the creative arts, is indeed about the details—especially how we negotiate the ones we do not expect.

In drafting this poem, I realized that I have never written about this because, I think, I was reluctant to separate the story and what needed to be *the poem*. Ted had a habit of reading my poetry drafts and drawing a line across the page—usually somewhere near the bottom third of the text. "All this earlier stuff," he would caution, "that's the stuff you tell the audience before you read it." For that reason, I thank the editors for the opportunity to include both the poem and a commentary in this volume.

At the St. Elizabeth Mammography Center

Lincoln, NE 2004

What I remember most
are the swirled dregs of coffee
peppered with loose grounds
in the bottom of the Styrofoam cup
I watched you drop into a repurposed
paper recycling bin near the automatic sliding door—

Your insistence was gentle, nearly nonchalant.
You waited because you knew I had no one else.
After the doctor dismissed me, I found you
cradling the cup between your palms,
ready to swap it for my trembling hands.
This wasn't part of our bargain,
teacher and student, but anything can change
in a moment; that is how we learn
the details are all that really matter.

Letter to TK: May 26, 2020

Someday, Sappho wrote,
they will remember us.

By reassembled quotation, tomb wrappings,
potsherds deciphered,
we have.

These strange almost-words
we now share
across our new, now-formal distance,
will they be remembered?

SARS-CoV 2   N95   PPE

No.

Not through eclipses,
ellipses, edits, erasures, sea rise, famine,
distraction.

To be forgettable, to be forgotten—
a kind of forgiveness.

But the deer you watched drink at the pond.

That there were deer.
That there were ponds.

Ordinary algae in summer.

Let them, o let them, join the spotted horses
painted on cave walls,
the slim girl assembled of colored pebbles
set into the floor of a palace.

Her implausible, lasting fragment
of looking, of hearing.

With such care, even now,
she carries
her pot filled with wine, water, and honey,
her banquet of fresh-baked wheat bread.

Here: let us eat with her,
in the back room she soon will return to.

. . .

"Letter to TK: May 26, 2020" was written the day I was invited
into this volume honoring Ted Kooser's long and immeasurable
generosity to us all—as poet, as teacher, as laureate, as exemplar,
as mentor and friend to so many. It's modeled, of course, on
Ted's own correspondence poems, particularly his exchanges
with Jim Harrison.

KWAME DAWES

The Chronicler of Sorrows

for Ted Kooser

Were I better at this, I would study almanacs,
chart the seasons, visit Ted Kooser on his farm
in midwinter, without invitation, and carry his
two by fours and barbwire rolls to the edge of his
land, and ask him the names of the birds
turning in the sky, or the yield of the corn crop,
or the number of people he has buried—farm people,
his people. Were I better at this I would
drink coffee in the quaint cafes in western tiny
towns, talk to those wary of me at first,
by then I would have learned the dialect of cattle,
of waterways, of the market, and we could talk
of Coronation market in Kingston, where their produce
would sell, undercutting the machete-armed farmer
from St. Anne's organic yield, the world turning
into a biblical economy of famine and plenty.
I would be the inside man, the reporter, the one
to trace the secret incantation of chemicals,
how they translate into college fees, new trucks,
mortgages; this would be my labor, my art, even.

I am not a better man. Instead I make up stories
like one who has been promised that his sayings
will become the source of proverbs, and he will be
remembered as the lone man, hooded, walking
across the sea-hardened beach where the tide
has receded so far, it appears a lie that soon

the bay will gleam with folds of the Atlantic;
stories like this one about the woman who one
day, without warning, declares herself tired
of words, and leaves her family for a convent
where everyone stays silent and eats vegetables
and stews, and artisan breads, and puts away
all devices that multiply words—she does this
for three weeks, pretending that she is tired
of speaking, but is really tired of hearing the sound
of her husband asking questions about heart,
and fear, and sorrow. So that when she returns
her depression is deeper, and she longs
for another month of empty silence,
for she learns that it is not so much words
she is escaping, but thought, the need
to make sense of things that have now
become too painful for thought. Of course,
she missed the beep of her phone, the friends
asking her where she is—that she missed.

And given the choice, wouldn't you choose
to be the guardian of the earth, instead of this
quite hapless chronicler of sorrows? There is a joke
here, and a proverb: "A man makes jokes
when he fears the joke is on him"—or something
such; next time I will include a pot. I know,
these days, that comedians are sad—why? Because,
they have the dull sorrow that makes funny
things unfunny, and no one beats a dead pan.

Fences

for Ted Kooser

I have collapsed two histories of arrival
into this alien landscape of wide fields,
big skies, and the lurking history of slaughter,
circling wagons, horse hoofs, and dust.
Even now I cannot shake off the clean
ethics of Hollywood from the language
of prairie history without the blunt
force of art: how corpses smell after
four days in the sun; how babies
left hungry vomit green bile and turn
to bones; how the sorrow and numb
despair enters the body's cells,
multiplying like a cancer from generation
to generation. And the truth is
these two collapsed histories
must be read through the filter
of the imperial anthem, the modern
white man's dogma of inventing
a race because it pays, sweet lord,
it pays. I think it was a snow-heavy
March morning, the campus empty

of students, when I met the spry old
poet, tender-eyed and gracious in everything,
who told me of the morning he had spent
mending the fences about his acreages,
deep in snow, under a brilliant sun,
gloved, pulling wires, digging deep
into ice, hauling timber, a kind of dogged
craft—the satisfaction in which came
the retelling—and the view of that long
unbroken line across the stretch of
uninterrupted snow, the drift covering
every trace of his effort, leaving
these elegant lines, even, going on
and on in a way a poet would call
stanzas, vanishing in the wide whiteness
of sky and land. Softly, softly, he spoke,
of the labor and the art, and I listened
with no understanding of the craft
of it, but fully seeing the end of it,
the gleam in his eyes for having
made it all, and having told it all,
so that a fence became everything
it had to be in that small moment,
a studied art. It may have been a year
after or it may have been a dream,
but I stood before a screen against
a wide wall, and the colors were blue
and white and sharp red of the truck,
and for hours I stared at the steady recording
of the making of a fence; no faces,
just the hands and the body of a man
in jeans and plaid shirt, yellow gloves
digging, pulling, dragging, nailing,
mending the fence, the camera not

moving, the sky barely reshaping itself
above it all, and the fence coming together.
I thought of the poet, of the coming of snow,
and I thought of myself standing outside
this world, and thinking of it as strange.
The poet lives with the calm of a man
at ease with memory. Perhaps, he, too
looks out over the white land and thinks
of what the discourse of deeds and treaties
has done to bodies that carry those cells
multiplying and multiplying their despair
and their wounds, and he, too,
grows weary of thinking of what might
have been. Memory carries its own price,
and the art of the American imagination
is the capacity to forget, to bully the body
into starting again: a field covered in snow;
mending fences by treating each log, each
bundle of wire as if it were just invented.
Such is the art of hegemony and holiness.
Providence is a cynic's comfort. What might
have been is an abstraction only if dreams
do not wound us even more deeply
than the lash. Someone stumbled
at line fifteen, and the rest is the blinding
of a blizzard. This is a shame; it is how,
I suppose, we erect our fences. But how
do I argue against the old manifest destiny,
the evidence of the triumphant
and the defeated? And, ah, here is why
Cecil Rhodes still strides over Oriel
College, whispering to the battered children
of his empire, "See? It pays, it pays, it pays!"

Source Acknowledgments

Hadara Bar-Nadav's "House" is from her book *The New Nudity* (Saturnalia Books, 2017).

Kwame Dawes's "The Chonicler of Sorrows" is from his book *Nebraska* (University of Nebraska Press, 2019).

"Fences" is from his and John Kinsella's book *Speak from Here to There* (Peepal Tree Press, 2016).

Jehanne Dubrow's "Pledge" was first published in the American Life in Poetry column (Fall 2020).

Crystal S. Gibbins's "Lake of the Woods" is from her book from *Now/Here* (Holy Cow! Press, 2017).

Dana Gioia's "Discovering Ted Kooser" is redacted from "Poetry Chronicle," *Hudson Review* 33.4 (Winter 1980–81).

Jonathan Greene's "One Light to Another" is from his book *Seeking Light: New & Selected Later Poems* (Broadstone Books, 2013).

Tami Haaland's "Sewing Room, 1973" is based on an earlier version published in *Ascent* (November 2019).

Andrea Hollander's "Old Snow" and "The Things Themselves" first appeared in *Midwest Quarterly 46:4* (Summer 2005).

Mark Irwin's "The smaller house" is forthcoming in *The Sun.*

Adrian Koesters's "Late Summer" is from her book *Three Days with the Long Moon* (BrickHouse Books, 2017).

Cody Lumpkin's "Old Man in the Hall of Nebraska Wildlife" was first published in *Weber: The Contemporary West* 31.1 (Fall 2014).

Rebecca Macijeski's "Time's Beard, His Closest Thing to Seasons" is forthcoming in *Sextant Review.*

Matt Mason's "Opening Night Rehearsal" is from his book *I Have a Poem the Size of the Moon* (Stephen F. Austin University Press, 2020).

Biljana Obradović's "Elegy for an Eastern Fallen Star" is from her book *Little Disruptions / Mali poremećaiji* (Niš Cultural Center Press, 2012).

Jessica Poli's "Holmes Lake" was first published on *poets.org* as the winner of the 2020 Wilbur Gaffney Award.

Naomi Shihab Nye's "Ted Kooser Is My President" is from her book *Honeybee* (Greenwillow Books, 2008).

Ivan Young's "Ferris Wheel" was first published in *Mantis* 18 (2020).

Contributors

Marco Abel is Willa Cather Professor of English at the University of Nebraska, where he's been chairing the English Department since 2014. Recipient of the American Academy in Berlin Prize in 2019, he is the author of *The Counter-Cinema of the Berlin School* (Camden House, 2013), which won the German Studies Association's Best Book Prize (2014), and *Violent Affect: Literature, Cinema, and Critique after Representation* (University of Nebraska Press, 2007), as well as coeditor of several volumes including *Celluloid Revolt: German Screen Cultures and the Long 1968* (Camden House, 2019) and of the University of Nebraska book series *Provocations*.

Jonis Agee is the author of twelve books of fiction, the most recent of which is the novel *The Bones of Paradise*. She shares her life with her husband, writer Brent Spencer, two adopted dogs, and a horse named Billy who also thinks he's a dog. She teaches in the English Department at the University of Nebraska–Lincoln.

Denise Banker has a PhD in English from the University of Nebraska and is the recipient of an Executive Director's Guest Fellowship from Civitella Ranieri Foundation, Umbertide, Italy. She is the author of the book-length collection of poems *Swimming the Colorado*, and her work has appeared in the ALAN *Review, Prairie Schooner, Midwest Quarterly, Natural Bridge*, and several anthologies. She taught English and creative writing at the University of Nebraska–Lincoln and Concordia University, Nebraska, and worked as publicist for Copper Canyon Press. Currently, she lives in the Pacific Northwest and serves as a public health educator and substance abuse prevention specialist for Jefferson County Public Health.

Hadara Bar-Nadav is a National Endowment for the Arts fellow and author of several award-winning collections of poetry, among them *The New Nudity, Lullaby (with Exit Sign), The Frame Called Ruin*, and others. She is also the coauthor of the best-selling textbook *Writing Poems*, 8th edition, and has individual poems published in the *Amer-*

ican Poetry Review, Believer, Kenyon Review, New Republic, Ploughshares, Tin House, and elsewhere. She is a professor of English and teaches in the MFA program at the University of Missouri–Kansas City.

Grace Bauer has published five books of poems—most recently, *MEAN/ TIME* (University of New Mexico Press) and a twentieth anniversary reissue of *The Women At the Well* (SFASU Press). She also coedited the anthology *Nasty Women Poets: An Unapologetic Anthology of Subversive Verse* (Lost Horse Press). Her collection *Unholy Heart: New & Selected Poems* is forthcoming from the University of Nebraska / Backwaters Press. She is the Aaron Douglas Emerita Professor of English and Creative Writing at the University of Nebraska.

Stephen Behrendt is the George Holmes Distinguished University Professor of English at the University of Nebraska. An international authority on British Romantic literature and culture, he is also a widely published poet whose fourth book-length collection, *Refractions,* appeared from Shechem Press in 2014. He delights in being an avid fan of the poetry of his longtime colleague and friend Ted Kooser.

Sarah A. Chavez, a mestiza born and raised in the California Central Valley, is the author of the poetry collections *Hands That Break & Scar* (Sundress Publications, 2017) and *All Day, Talking* (dancing girl press, 2014), and has also published in *Xicanx: Mexican American Writers of the 21st Century, Diode,* and *Hotel Amerika.* Her new poetry project, *Halfbreed Helene Navigates the Whole,* received a 2019–20 Tacoma Artists Initiative Award. Chavez teaches creative writing and Latinx/Chicanx-focused courses at the University of Washington–Tacoma, serves as poetry coordinator for Best of the Net Anthology, and is a member of the Macondo Writers Workshop.

Sharon Chmielarz was born and raised in Mobridge, South Dakota, three miles from the Missouri River. She graduated from the University of Minnesota and has since lived and worked in the Twin Cities. Her latest, twelfth, book of poetry is *The J Horoscope,* 2019. *Kirkus Reviews* named her books *The Widow's House* and *The J Horoscope* (Brighthorse Books) one of the 100 Best Books of 2016 and 2019, respectively. You can visit her at www.sharonchmielarz.com.

Gerald Costanzo is the author of *Regular Haunts: New and Previous Poems* (University of Nebraska Press, 2018) and eight other collections of poems. He has edited five anthologies of contemporary poetry and has been the recipient of two Pushcart Prizes, two National Endowment for the Arts Creative Writing Fellowships, as well as other awards. A graduate of Harvard and of the Writing Seminars at Johns Hopkins, he has been a professor of English at Carnegie Mellon University since 1970.

James Crews is the author of four books of poetry: *The Book of What Stays* (winner of the Prairie Schooner Book Prize), *Telling My Father*, *Bluebird*, and *Every Waking Moment*. He is also the editor of two anthologies: *Healing the Divide: Poems of Kindness and Connection* and *How to Love the World: Poems of Gratitude and Hope*. He lives on part of an organic farm in Vermont with his husband.

Barbara Crooker is a poetry editor for *Italian-Americana* and author of twelve chapbooks and nine full-length books of poetry. *Some Glad Morning* (Pitt Poetry Series, University of Pittsburgh Press, 2019) is the latest. Her awards include the W. B. Yeats Society of New York Award, the Thomas Merton Poetry of the Sacred Award, and three Pennsylvania Council fellowships in literature. Her work appears in literary journals and anthologies, including *Common Wealth: Contemporary Poets on Pennsylvania* and *The Bedford Introduction to Literature*. She has been on the *Writer's Almanac* fifty-some times, and featured in Ted Kooser's column American Life in Poetry.

James Daniels's recent books include *Rowing Inland* and *Street Calligraphy* (poetry), *The Perp Walk* (short fiction), and the anthology he edited with M. L. Liebler, RESPECT: *The Poetry of Detroit Music*. A native of Detroit, he currently lives in Pittsburgh, where he teaches at Carnegie Mellon University.

Todd Davis is a former fellow of the Black Earth Institute and the author of six collections of poetry, most recently *Native Species* (2019) and *Winterkill* (2016), both published by Michigan State University Press. His writing has won the Foreword INDIES Book of the Year Bronze and Silver Awards, the Midwest Book Award, the Gwendolyn Brooks Poetry Prize, the Chautauqua Editors Prize, and the Bloomsburg University Book Prize. He teaches environmental studies, American literature, and creative writing at Pennsylvania State University's Altoona College.

Kwame Dawes is the author of twenty-two books of poetry, including *Nebraska* (2020), and numerous books of fiction, criticism, and essays.

He is Glenna Luschei Editor of *Prairie Schooner* and teaches at the University of Nebraska and the Pacific MFA Program. He is director of the African Poetry Book Fund and artistic director of the Calabash International Literary Festival. Dawes is a chancellor of the Academy of American Poets and a fellow of the Royal Society of Literature. His awards include an Emmy, the Forward Poetry Prize, a Guggenheim Fellowship, and the Windham Campbell Prize for Poetry. In 2021, he was named editor of American Life in Poetry.

Jehanne Dubrow is the author of seven poetry collections and a book of creative nonfiction. Her work has appeared in *Poetry, New England Review,* and *Southern Review.* She is a professor of creative writing at the University of North Texas.

Saddiq Dzukogi was born in Minna, Nigeria. He is the author of *Your Crib, My Qibla* (University of Nebraska Press, 2021) and the chapbook *Inside the Flower Room,* a selection of the New Generation African Poets Chapbook series. His poems have appeared in *Prairie Schooner, Kenyon Review, World Literature Today, Oxford Poetry, Oxford Review of Books, Southeast Review,* and others. He is currently a PhD student in English at the University of Nebraska, where he received the Vreeland Award for Poetry.

Dan Gerber is the author of nine collections of poetry, most recently *Particles: New & Selected Poems* (Copper Canyon Press 2017), three novels, a book of short stories, and two books of nonfiction. His work has appeared in the *Nation,* the *New Yorker, Poetry, Partisan Review, Caliban, Narrative,* and *Best American Poetry.* His books have received Book of the Year Awards from Foreword Magazine and The Society of Midland Authors, a Michigan Notable Book Award, and The Mark Twain Award. He lives with his wife, Debbie, and their menagerie, domestic and wild, near Santa Ynez, California.

Crystal S. Gibbins is a Canadian American writer, founder/editor of *Split Rock Review,* editor of the anthology *Rewilding: Poems for the Environment,* and author of *Now/Here,* winner of the 2017 Northeastern Minnesota Book Award for Poetry. She holds a PhD in English from the University of Nebraska. Her poetry and comics appear in *Coffee House Writers Project, Hobart, North American Review, Verse Daily, Writer's Almanac,* and elsewhere. Originally from the Northwest Angle and Islands in Lake of the Woods (Minnesota/Ontario), she lives on the south shore of Lake Superior in northern Wisconsin. For more information, visit www.crystalgibbins.com.

Dana Gioia, a poet and critic, has published five full-length collections of verse, most recently *99 Poems: New & Selected* (2016), which won the Poets' Prize. His collection *Interrogations at Noon* (2001) received the American Book Award. He has also published four critical collections, including *Can Poetry Matter?*, which was a finalist for the National Book Critics Circle Award. He has written four opera libretti and collaborated with musicians in genres from classical to jazz and rock. For six years Gioia served as chair of the National Endowment for the Arts. He also served as California Poet Laureate from 2015 to 2019. He taught poetry and arts leadership at University of Southern California as the Judge Widney Professor of Poetry and Public Culture and now divides his time between Los Angeles and Sonoma County.

Diane Glancy is professor emerita at Macalester College. Currently she teaches in the low-residency MFA program at Carlow University. Her latest book, *Island of the Innocent, a Consideration of the Book of Job*, was published in 2020 by Turtle Point Press. Forthcoming books are *A Line of Driftwood, the Ada Blackjack Story* (Turtle Point) and *Still Moving, How the Road, the Land and the Sacred Shape a Life* (Broadleaf Books, Fortress Press). The rest of her books and awards are on her website www.dianeglancy.com.

Sally Green's latest collection of poems is *Full Immersion* (Expedition Press, 2014). She has been copublisher of Brooding Heron Press for nearly forty years. Honors include a grant from Artist Trust and a Stanley W. Lindberg Editor's Award for excellence. Sally produced two chapbooks by Ted Kooser: *Out of That Moment: Twenty-one Years of Valentines* and *Together*, both from handset type, printed on a one-hundred-year-old platen press.

Samuel Green's most recent poetry collection is *Disturbing the Light* (Carnegie Mellon University, 2020). Honors include fellowships from the National Endowment for the Arts and Artist Trust, a term as the inaugural poet laureate of Washington, and an honorary doctorate from Seattle University.

Jonathan Greene is the author of thirty-seven books. Among his recent titles are *Seeking Light, New and Selected Poems* (2013), *Anecdotage: Everyday Epiphanies* (autobiographical prose, 2015), *Gists Orts Shards* (a commonplace book, 2018), *Afloat* (poems, 2018), all from Broadstone Books.

Tami Haaland is the author of three poetry collections, most recently *What Does Not Return* (Lost Horse Press, 2018). Her poems have appeared in many periodicals and anthologies, including *Consequence, American Journal of Poetry, Ascent, Ecopoetry Anthology,* and *Healing the Divide.* Her work has also been featured on *Slowdown, Writer's Almanac, Verse Daily,* and American Life in Poetry. Haaland teaches at Montana State University–Billings.

Twyla M. Hansen was Nebraska's State Poet from 2013 to 2018. She codirects the *Poetry from the Plains* website and has conducted readings/writing workshops through Humanities Nebraska since 1993. Her newest book, *Rock • Tree • Bird,* won the 2018 WILLA Literary Award and Nebraska Book Award. She has six previous books of poetry, including *Potato Soup,* which won the 2012 Nebraska Book Award and was selected as a Notable Nebraska 150 Book in 2017. Her writing is published in the Academy of American Poets, Poetry Foundation, Poetry Out Loud, *Prairie Schooner, Midwest Quarterly, Organization & Environment, Encyclopedia of the Great Plains,* and many more.

Judith Harris is the author of *Atonement* (LSU Press), *The Bad Secret* (LSU Press), *Night Garden* (Tiger Bark), and the critical book *Signifying Pain: Constructing and Healing the Self through Writing* (SUNY). Her poetry has appeared in the *Nation,* the *Atlantic, New Republic, Slate, Southern Review, Hudson Review, Ploughshares,* and American Life in Poetry, and her essays and interviews with poets have appeared in the *Writer's Chronicle, Midwest Quarterly, Prairie Schooner,* and Graywolf's *After Confession: Poetry as Autobiography.* She publishes on psychoanalysis and literature and is working on a forthcoming book about grief in the contemporary elegy.

Jeffrey Harrison is the author of six books of poetry, most recently *Between Lakes* (Four Way Books, 2020). His previous book, *Into Daylight,* (2014), won the Dorset Prize from Tupelo Press, while *Incomplete Knowledge* (2006) was runner-up for the Poets' Prize. His first book, *The Singing Underneath,* was selected by James Merrill for the National Poetry Series in 1987. He has received fellowships from the Guggenheim Foundation and the National Endowment for the Arts, and his poems have appeared widely in magazines and anthologies, including *Best American Poetry* and *The Pushcart Prize* volumes, and been featured in Ted Kooser's column American Life in Poetry.

Karen Head is the author of *Disrupt This!: MOOCs and the Promises of Technology* and five poetry collections (*Lost on Purpose, Sassing, My Paris Year, Shadow Boxes,* and *On Occasion: Four Poets, One Year*). Her work appears in many journals and anthologies, and she was the 2010 Oxford International Women's Festival Poetry Prize–winner. She creates digital poetry and has exhibited several acclaimed digital poetry projects. Her work has been translated for German, French, and Mandarin publications. She is the editor of the international poetry journal *Atlanta Review,* is the Waffle House Poet Laureate, and an associate professor at Georgia Tech.

Robert Hedin is the author, translator, and editor of two dozen books of poetry and prose, most recently *At the Great Door of Morning: Selected Poems and Translations* (Copper Canyon Press). He is co-founder and former director of the Anderson Center, a residential artist retreat, and lives in Frontenac, Minnesota.

Jane Hirshfield's most recent, ninth, poetry collection is *Ledger* (Knopf, 2020). The founder of #PoetsForScience, Hirshfield is also the author of two now-classic books of essays, *Nine Gates* and *Ten Windows.* A finalist for the National Book Critics Circle Award, long-listed for the National Book Award, and winner of the Poetry Center and California Book Awards, Hirshfield's other honors include fellowships from the Guggenheim and Rockefeller foundations, the National Endowment for the Arts, and ten selections for *The Best American Poetry.* A former chancellor of the Academy of American Poets, she was inducted in 2019 into the American Academy of Arts and Sciences.

Andrea Hollander is the author of five poetry collections and the recipient of numerous honors and awards, including two Pushcart Prizes (poetry and literary nonfiction) and two fellowships from the National Endowment for the Arts. In 2011, after more than three decades living in the Arkansas Ozark Mountains, where she ran a bed and breakfast for fifteen years and served as the writer-in-residence at Lyon College for twenty-two, she moved to Portland, Oregon, where she founded the Ambassador Writing Seminars. Her website is www.andreahollander.net.

Mark Irwin's ten collections of poetry include the recently published *Shimmer* (2020), winner of the Philip Levine Prize for Poetry, *A Passion According to Green* (2017), *American Urn: New & Selected Poems (1987–2014)*, *Tall If* (2009), and *Bright Hunger* (2004). He recently completed a long translation project entitled *Zanzibar: Selected Poems and Letters of Arthur Rimbaud*, with an afterword by Alain Borer. Recognition for his work includes a Discovery/The Nation Award, two Colorado Book Awards, four Pushcart Prizes, the James Wright Poetry Award, and fellowships from the Fulbright, Lilly Endowment, and the National Endowment for the Arts.

Stuart Kestenbaum is the author of five collections of poems, most recently *How to Start Over* (Deerbrook Editions 2019), and a collection of essays *The View from Here* (Brynmorgen Press). He's the host of the Maine Public Radio program *Poems from Here* and was the host/curator of the podcast *Make/Time*. He is currently serving as Maine's Poet Laureate.

Adrian Koesters holds an MFA in poetry from Pacific Lutheran University and a PhD in English from the University of Nebraska. She is the author of the poetry collections *Many Parishes* and *Three Days with the Long Moon* and the novels *Union Square* and *Miraculous Medal*. Her work has appeared in *Prairie Schooner, Berkeley Review, Gettysburg Review*, and elsewhere. She was graduate assistant editor for the column American Life in Poetry from 2010 to 2011, taught creative writing at UNL and Creighton University, and is retired from the University of Nebraska system. She lives in Omaha.

Cody Lumpkin is a visiting assistant professor of English at Marshall University, where he teaches courses in literature and film. His poetry has been published in *Tar River Poetry, Weber: The Contemporary West*, and *South Dakota Review*. He earned his PhD in English at the University of Nebraska, where he served as a senior poetry reader and book prize coordinator for *Prairie Schooner*. During his time as a graduate student at Nebraska, he would often pass Ted Kooser in the corridors of Andrews Hall and tried his best to give a nonchalant, unobtrusive nod as they passed each other.

Jill McCabe Johnson's poetry books include *Revolutions We'd Hoped We'd Outgrown*, a Clara Johnson Award in Women's Literature finalist, and *Diary of the One Swelling Sea*, a Nautilus Books Silver Award winner, plus the chapbooks *Pendulum* and *Borderlines*. Jill holds a PhD in English from the University of Nebraska, where she was the Louise Van Sickle Fellow in Poetry, and an MFA from the Rainier Writing Workshop, where she was the Deborah Tall Fellow. Honors include support from the National Endowment for the Humanities, Artist Trust, and Hedgebrook. Jill founded Wandering Aengus Press and teaches at Skagit Valley College.

Rebecca Macijeski holds a PhD from the University of Nebraska and an MFA from the Vermont College of Fine Arts. She has worked for Ted Kooser's American Life in Poetry column and as an assistant editor in poetry for the literary journals *Prairie Schooner* and *Hunger Mountain*. Her poems have appeared in *Missouri Review, Poet Lore, Cincinnati Review, Nimrod, Journal, Sycamore Review, Fairy Tale Review, Puerto del Sol, Conduit, Gargoyle*, and many others. Rebecca is currently creative writing program coordinator and assistant professor at Northwestern State University.

Freya Manfred is the author of nine books of poetry, most recently *Loon in Late November Water* (Red Dragonfly Press, 2018). Manfred's poetry won a Harvard/Radcliffe Fellowship, an NEA Grant, and the 2009 Midwest Booksellers Choice Award. Her memoir *Frederick Manfred: A Daughter Remembers*, was nominated for a Minnesota Book Award and an Iowa Historical Society Award. Her sons, award-winning artists Bly and Rowan Pope, are celebrated in her memoir, *Raising Twins: A True Life Adventure*. She's married to screenwriter Thomas Pope.

Matt Mason is the Nebraska State Poet and executive director of the Nebraska Writers Collective. He has run poetry programs for the U.S. State Department in Nepal, Romania, Botswana, and Belarus. Mason is the recipient of a Pushcart Prize, and his work can be found in magazines and anthologies including Ted Kooser's American Life in Poetry column. The author of *Things We Don't Know We Don't Know* (Backwaters Press, 2006) and *The Baby That Ate Cincinnati* (Stephen F. Austin University Press, 2013), Matt is based out of Omaha with his wife, the poet Sarah McKinstry-Brown, and daughters Sophia and Lucia.

Sarah McKinstry-Brown, winner of an Academy of American Poets Prize and two Nebraska Book Awards, is the author of *Cradling Monsoons* (Blue Light Press, 2010) and *This Bright Darkness* (Black Lawrence

Press, 2019). Her poems can be found everywhere from West Virginia's standardized tests to literary journals such as *Rattle, South Dakota Review,* and *Smartish Pace.* Most recently, Sarah's work was featured in *Nebraska Poetry: A Sesquicentennial Anthology.* She teaches writing at the University of Nebraska at Omaha and lives in Ponca Hills with her two daughters and current Nebraska State Poet Matt Mason.

Michelle Menting has received honors and awards from Sewanee, Bread Loaf, the National Park Service, and the Maine Literary Awards, among others. Her writing has appeared in numerous magazines, including *Diagram, Southeast Review, Fourth River,* and *Cimarron Review,* and her poems have been featured in the American Life in Poetry column, *New Poetry from the Midwest,* and *Verse Daily.* Her most recent poetry collection is *Leaves Surface Like Skin* (Terrapin Books). She holds an MFA in poetry and nonfiction and earned her PhD at the University of Nebraska. She lives in Maine and teaches at the University of Southern Maine.

Amelia María de la Luz Montes is associate professor of English and Ethnic Studies at the University of Nebraska. As a Fulbright Scholar, she taught and conducted research at the University of Novi Sad, Serbia. Her publications and teaching include nineteenth-century to contemporary Chicana/U.S. Latina literatures, LGBTQ literatures, and creative writing. Her Penguin Classics edition of Ruiz de Burton's *Who Would Have Thought It?* was recognized by the Association of American Publishers. Her essay "Defining La Rumorosa and Borderlands" (*Fifth Wednesday Journal,* 2018) was nominated for a Pushcart Prize; her short story "La Omaha Mariachi Dyke" appears in the *Afro-Hispanic Review.*

Trey Moody was born and raised in San Antonio, Texas. His first book, *Thought That Nature* (Sarabande Books, 2014), won the Kathryn A. Morton Prize in Poetry. His more recent poems have appeared in *Believer, Conduit, Ecotone, Gulf Coast,* and *New England Review.* He teaches at Creighton University and lives with his daughter in Omaha, Nebraska.

Maria Nazos's poetry, translations, and essays are published in the *New Yorker, North American Review,* and *Mid-American Review.* She is the author of *A Hymn That Meanders* (Wising Up Press, 2011) and the chapbook *Still Life* (dancing girl press, 2016). Her work received a fellowship from the Virginia Center for the Creative Arts and a Tennessee Williams Scholarship from the Sewanee Writers' Conference. A graduate of UNL's English PhD program, she served as graduate assistant for Ted Kooser's American Life in Poetry column. To this day, she considers Ted to be her Gramps. She can be found at www.marianazos.com.

Naomi Shihab Nye is the Young People's Poet Laureate (Poetry Foundation) until 2022 and has been editor of the *New York Times Magazine* poem for the past year. She is on the faculty at Texas State University, and her most recent books are *Cast Away, The Tiny Journalist,* and *Voices in the Air.*

Debra Nystrom has published four books of poetry: *A Quarter Turn, Torn Sky, Bad River Road,* and most recently *Night Sky Frequencies.* Her poetry, fiction, and nonfiction have appeared in *Best American Poetry, New Yorker, Ploughshares, Kenyon Review, Slate, American Poetry Review, Narrative, Conjunctions, Yale Review,* and elsewhere. She teaches in the MFA program at the University of Virginia.

Biljana D. Obradović is a poet, translator, critic, and professor of English at Xavier University. She received a BA from Belgrade University, an MFA from Virginia Commonwealth University, and a PhD in English from the University of Nebraska. She has published four collections of poems, including *Incognito* (2017); several books of translations of poems—into English from Serbian (by Bratislav Milanović, Zvonko Karanović) and into Serbian from English (by John Gery, Stanley Kunitz, Patrizia de Rachewiltz, Bruce Weigl, and Niyi Osundare); two anthologies (*Fives* and *Cat Painters: An Anthology of Contemporary Serbian Poetry*); and a collection of essays by Philip Dacey, *Heavenly Muse: Essays on Poetry.*

Suzanne Ohlmann is a writer and nurse who manages rural heart-failure patients. She received an MFA from Wilkes University, a BS from Columbia University, and a Bachelor of Music from St. Olaf College. She lives in both her native Nebraska and San Antonio, Texas. A contributor to *Texas Monthly Magazine,* her essays have been published by the Associated Press, *Intima: The Journal of Narrative Medicine,* and *Longreads: the Best Longform Stories on the Web.* Her first book, *Shadow Migration,* will be published by the University of Nebraska Press in 2022.

Linda Parsons is a poet, playwright, and editor. She is the poetry editor at Madville Publishing and coordinates WordStream, WDVX-FM's weekly reading/performance series, with Stellasue Lee. Linda's poetry has appeared in *Georgia Review, Iowa Review, Prairie Schooner, Southern Poetry Review, Chattahoochee Review, Baltimore Review,* and *Shenandoah,* among many others. *Candescent* is her fifth poetry collection (Iris Press, 2019). She is the reviews editor for *Pine Mountain Sand & Gravel* and the copy editor for *Chapter 16,* the literary website of Humanities Tennessee.

Amy Plettner is the author of the poetry collections *Undoing Orion's Belt* and *Points of Entry.* She holds an MFA from the University of Nebraska at Omaha. Her poetry has been published in a variety of journals and anthologies, most recently *Misbehaving Nebraskans; Nebraska Poetry: A Sesquicentennial Anthology* 1867–2017; *Bared,* a Les Femmes Folles Book; *burntdistrict;* and *Rattle.*

Jessica Poli is the author of four chapbooks, most recently *Canyons* (Bat-Cat Press, 2018). She is a PhD student at the University of Nebraska, founder and editor of *Birdfeast,* and assistant poetry editor at *Prairie Schooner.*

JC Reilly writes across genres to keep things interesting. She is the author of *La Petite Mort,* a poetry chapbook, and *What Magick May Not Alter,* a Southern Gothic novel-in-verse. She is also the 2020 winner of the *Sow's Ear Poetry Review* Prize for her poemoir chapbook *Amo e Canto,* which will be published in 2021. When she's not writing, she plays tennis, crochets, and practices her Italian. A Louisiana native, she lives in Marietta, Georgia, and serves as the managing editor of the *Atlanta Review.* Follow her @Aishatonu.

Todd Robinson is an assistant professor in the Writer's Workshop at the University of Nebraska–Omaha. He has published two books of poetry, most recently *Mass for Shut-Ins* (Backwaters Press). He holds a PhD in English from the University of Nebraska, and his work has graced the pages of *Sugar House Review, Weber—the Contemporary West, Cortland Review,* and *Hayden's Ferry Review.*

Marjorie Saiser's *The Print the Whales Make: New & Selected* will be published in 2021 in Ted Kooser's series at the University of Nebraska Press. Saiser's poems can be found in Kooser's American Life in Poetry column, *Rattle, Writer's Almanac, Poet Lore, bosque, Briar Cliff*

Review, Chattahoochee Review, Prairie Schooner, and at poetmarge. com. Saiser is the author of seven books of poetry, coeditor of two anthologies, and winner of the Willa Award in 2014 for *Losing the Ring in the River.*

Mark Sanders is a Nebraska native, currently living in east Texas where he is associate dean of Liberal and Applied Arts at Stephen F. Austin State University. Among his recent works are *In a Good Time: Poems* (WSC Press, 2019), *Landscapes, with Horses* (SFASU Press, 2018), and *The Weight of the Weather: Regarding the Poetry of Ted Kooser* (SFASU Press, 2017). He has received a Western Heritage Award (2019), three Nebraska Book Awards (2016, 2018, 2019), and the Spur Award (2020). In 2007, he received the Mildred Bennett Award for fostering Nebraska's literary heritage.

Timothy Schaffert is the author of six novels, most recently *The Perfume Thief* (Knopf Doubleday). He has worked as an editor of newspapers and literary journals and is the editor of *You Will Never See Any God: Stories by Ervin D. Krause* (University of Nebraska Press) and project director for the Trans-Mississippi and International Exposition Digital Archive. His fiction has been adapted into film, theater, performance art, and fashion. He writes the column The Eccentricities of Gentlemen for *Enchanted Living* magazine, and he is the director of creative writing at the University of Nebraska.

Katie Schmid's first book of poems, *Nowhere,* is forthcoming from the University of New Mexico Press in Fall 2021.

Faith Shearin's books of poetry include *The Owl Question* (May Swenson Award), *Moving the Piano, Telling the Bees, Orpheus, Turning* (Dogfish Poetry Prize), *Darwin's Daughter,* and *Lost Language* (forthcoming, Press 53). She has received awards from Yaddo, the National Endowment for the Arts, the Barbara Deming Memorial Fund, and the Fine Arts Work Center in Provincetown. Recent work has been featured on the *Writer's Almanac* and included in American Life in Poetry.

Peggy Shumaker writes poems and nonfiction. Her most recent book is *Cairn: New and Selected Poems and Prose.* Every encounter she has had with Ted Kooser has involved poetry, laughter, and delight. She'd split an order of fries with him anytime.

Christine Stewart-Nuñez, South Dakota's Poet Laureate, is the author of seven books, most recently *Untrussed* (University of New Mexico

Press, 2016) and *Bluewords Greening* (Terrapin Books, 2016), and winner of the 2018 Whirling Prize. As a professor at South Dakota State University, Christine's work has earned recognition, most recently a Woman of Distinction Award (2020) and an Outstanding Experiential Learning Educator Award (2019). She served on the South Dakota State Poetry Society's board of directors from 2012 to 2018 and edited its poetry magazine, *Pasque Petals.* She's also the founder of South Dakota's Women Poets Collective. Find out more at christinestewartnunez.com.

Mary K. Stillwell earned her PhD in English from the University of Nebraska. Her work has appeared in *Paris Review, Massachusetts Review, Prairie Schooner, South Dakota Review, New York Quarterly,* and other publications. She is the author of *The Life and Poetry of Ted Kooser* (University of Nebraska Press). Her books include *Reasonable Doubts, Maps & Destinations, Fallen Angels,* and *Moving to Malibu.* Her coedited anthology of Nebraska poetry, *Nebraska Presence,* was the 2018 One Book One Nebraska selection. She received a 2018 Nebraska Arts Council Individual Artist Fellowship.

Joyce Sutphen grew up on a small farm in Stearns County, Minnesota. Her first collection of poems, *Straight Out of View,* won the Barnard New Women Poets Prize. Her recent books are *The Green House* (Salmon Poetry, 2017) and *Carrying Water to the Field: New and Selected Poems* (University of Nebraska Press, 2019). She is the second Minnesota Poet Laureate, succeeding Robert Bly, and she is professor emerita of literature and creative writing at Gustavus Adolphus College in St. Peter, Minnesota.

Mark Vinz is professor emeritus of English at Minnesota State University–Moorhead. From 1971 to 1981 he was also the president of Plains Distribution Service and editor of the poetry journal *Dacotah Territory* and from 1973 to 2007 the editor of Dacotah Territory Press. His poems, prose poems, stories, and essays have appeared in several magazines and anthologies. His most recent books are *Permanent Record* (poems) and a memoir, *Man of the House: Scenes from a '50s Childhood.* He has also coedited several collections, including *Inheriting the Land: Contemporary Voices from the Midwest* and *The Party Train: A Collection of North American Prose Poetry.*

Hope Wabuke is a poet, writer, and an assistant professor of English and creative writing at the University of Nebraska. She is the author of several collections of poetry and the forthcoming memoir *Please Don't Kill My Black Son Please*; she has also won awards from the National Endowment for the Arts, the Barbara Deming Memorial Fund for Women Writers, Cave Canem, VONA, and elsewhere.

Stacey Waite is associate professor of English at the University of Nebraska and is the author of *Choke* (winner of the Frank O'Hara Prize for Poetry), *Love Poem to Androgyny*, *the lake has no saint*, and *Butch Geography*. Waite's essays on the teaching of writing have appeared most recently in *College Composition and Communication* and *Writing on the Edge*. Waite's newest book is *Teaching Queer: Radical Possibilities for Writing and Knowing* (University of Pittsburgh Press, 2017).

Connie Wanek has relished a wonderful correspondence with Ted Kooser over the last fifteen or so years. While he was U.S. Poet Laureate, Mr. Kooser named Wanek a Witter Bynner Fellow of the Library of Congress. She's had five books of poems published, most recently *Consider the Lilies: Mrs. God Poems*. She also coauthored a book of children's poetry with Mr. Kooser, which is forthcoming from Candlewick Press.

Sandra Yannone received her PhD from the University of Nebraska in 1998. Salmon Poetry published her debut collection, *Boats for Women*, in 2019; the manuscript was her dissertation, chaired by Hilda Raz. Salmon Poetry will publish her book, *The Glass Studio*, in 2022. Her poems and book reviews have appeared in numerous journals including *Ploughshares*, *Poetry Ireland Review*, *Prairie Schooner*, *Sweet*, *Live Encounters*, *Women's Review of Books*, *Impossible Archetype*, and *Lambda Literary Review*. She has written several essays on the intersections between poetry and social justice for *Works in Progress*. She hosts Cultivating Voices LIVE Poetry on Facebook on Sundays. Visit her at www.sandrayannone.com.

Ivan Young completed his PhD at the University of Nebraska in May of 2019 and is the author of *Smell of Salt, Ghost of Rain* (Brickhouse Books) and *A Shape in the Waves* (Stepping Stones Press). His most recent work can be found in *Minnesota Review*, *Mantis*, *RHINO*, and *Third Wednesday*. Ivan currently works as communications coordinator of the Preschool Development Grant at Nebraska Children and Families Foundation. He lives in Omaha with his wife and two children.

Rosemary Zumpfe is a poet and artist living in Lincoln, Nebraska. She has an MA in art from the University of Missouri and a PhD in English from the University of Nebraska. Her poems have appeared in *Nebraska Presence*, the anthology *Times of Sorrow, Times of Grace*, and various literary journals. She teaches drawing, painting, and art history at Southeast Community College.